Thomas Guthrie

Speaking to the Heart or Sermons for the People

Thomas Guthrie

Speaking to the Heart or Sermons for the People

ISBN/EAN: 9783743312333

Manufactured in Europe, USA, Canada, Australia, Japa

Cover: Foto ©Thomas Meinert / pixelio.de

Manufactured and distributed by brebook publishing software (www.brebook.com)

Thomas Guthrie

Speaking to the Heart or Sermons for the People

EAKING TO THE HEART

OR

SERMONS FOR THE PEOPLE

BY

THOMAS GUTHRIE, D.D

AUTHOR OF "THE GOSPEL IN EZEKIEL," ETC

LONDON
ALEXANDER, STRAHAN & CO
1862

CONTENTS.

	PAGE
I. NEGLECTED WARNINGS	1
II. FEAR, THE FRUIT OF DIVINE FORGIVENESS,	20
III. THE UNDECAYING POWER AND GRACE OF GOD	38
IV. THE GRACE OF FAITH	57
V. THE GRACE OF FAITH	74
VI. THE GRACE OF HOPE	91
VII. THE GRACE OF CHARITY	109
VIII. THE GOOD FIGHT	127
IX. THE TRIAL AND TRIUMPH OF FAITH	143
X. THE TRUE TEST	163
XI. SPIRITUAL VISION	183
XII. THE APOSTATE	201

The Author of this Volume thinks it right to state that its Name is not of his choosing. Owing to a misunderstanding it was advertised by his esteemed friend the Publisher under the title of "Speaking to the Heart," and this title is allowed to stand, as the altering of it now would lead to confusion.

EDINBURGH, *1st December*, 1862.

I.

NEGLECTED WARNINGS.

"Gray hairs are here and there upon him, yet he knoweth not."
—Hosea vii. 9.

FIRE low—the order which generals have often given to their men before fighting began—suits the pulpit not less than the battle-field. The mistake common both to soldiers and speakers is to shoot too high, over people's heads; missing, by a want of directness and plainness, both the persons they preach to and the purpose they preach for. So did not the prophet Nathan, when, having told his story of the little ewe lamb, and kindled David's indignation, he fixed his eyes on the king to say, Thou art the man. So did not the Baptist, when, recognising in the crowd Pharisees swollen with pride and rich with the spoil of orphans, he cried, O generation of vipers, who hath warned you to flee from the wrath to come? And, though with speech less blunt and rude and unpolite withal, as some might say, so did not the great apostle of the Gentiles, but directed his addresses, like arrows, to the hearts and habits, the bosoms and business of his audience. In Athens, full of false gods, he proclaimed the true one; in Corinth he denounced the vices which made her name so infamous. Before the Hebrews, who clung so tenaciously to the sacrifices of lambs, bulls, and goats, he set forth the Lamb of God, which taketh away the sin of the world—like an expert physician applying to each disease its own direct and appropriate remedy.

Arraigned at a judgment bar, it furnished him with a topic of discourse. He proclaimed the judgment to come, and, with the skill of an orator and the courage of a martyr, preached to an intemperate and unrighteous judge of temperance and righteousness, till, as the captive flashed and thundered from the bar, the judge on the bench grew pale and trembled. In this he followed the example of Him, the Prince of Preachers, whom the common people, enchanted and enchained with his speech, heard gladly—speaking, in the judgment even of his enemies, as never man spake.

With matter divine and manner human, our Lord descended to the level of the humblest of the crowd, lowering himself to their understandings, and winning his way into their hearts by borrowing his topics from familiar circumstances and the scenes around him. Be it a boat, a plank, a rope, a beggar's rags, an imperial robe, we would seize on anything to save a drowning man; and in his anxiety to save poor sinners, to rouse their fears, their love, their interest, to make them understand and feel the truth, our Lord pressed everything—art and nature, earth and heaven —into his service. Creatures of habit, the servants if not the slaves of form, we invariably select our text from some book of the Sacred Scriptures. He took a wider, freer range; and, instead of keeping to the unvarying routine of text and sermon with formal divisions, it were well, perhaps, that we sometimes ventured to follow his example; for may it not be to the naturalness of their addresses and their striking out from the beaten path of texts and sermons, to their plain speaking and home-thrusts, to their direct appeals and homespun arguments, that our street and lay preachers owe perhaps not a little of their power?

Illustrating the words of the great English dramatist—

> " Finds tongues in trees, books in the running brooks,
> Sermons in stones, and good in everything,"

our Lord found many a topic of discourse in the scenes around him; even the humblest objects shone in his hands as I have seen a fragment of broken glass or earthenware, as it caught the sunbeam, light up, flashing like a diamond. With the stone of Jacob's well for a pulpit, and its water for a text, he preached salvation to the Samaritan woman. A little child, which he takes from its mother's side, and holds up blushing in his arms before the astonished audience, is his text for a sermon on humility. A husbandman on a neighbouring height between him and the sky, who strides with long and measured steps over the field he sows, supplies a text from which he discourses on the Gospel and its effects on different classes of hearers. In a woman baking; in two women who sit by some cottage door grinding at the mill; in an old, strong fortalice perched on a rock, whence it looks across the brawling torrent to the ruined and roofless gable of a house swept away by mountain floods—Jesus found texts. From the birds that sung above his head, and the lilies that blossomed at his feet, he discoursed on the care of God —these his text, and Providence his theme; and with gray hairs on our own head and hoary heads around, we feel that his practice justifies us in making these our text; and addressing you, as I proceed to do, from these words—"Gray hairs are here and there upon him, yet he knoweth not."

I. Gray hairs are a sign of decay.

Giving a mane to the lion, antlers to the hart, to the males among birds a brighter plumage, and among four-footed beasts a bolder carriage and a bigger form, God, the maker of all, has distinguished the sexes, not only among mankind, but among the higher orders of the lower animals. He had a wise purpose in this. A God of order and not of confusion, he has for wise purposes also given distinctive features to the different periods of human life, from the cradle onwards to the grave. In roaming over the mountains, we often find on the tops of all but peaked and picturesque ranges, a level space—a table-land, as it is called, between the ascent from one valley and the descent into another, where the water, having no run, gathers into lonely tarns, or stagnates in a black morass. Human life between the ages of forty and fifty presents such a level. Travelling onward with little change in our appearance, in our powers of body or of mind; after growth has ceased and before decay has begun; ere the signs of youth have entirely left us or those of age have come; arrived at full maturity, with waste and supply in perfect balance, it were hard to say whether we are yet ascending from the cradle, or, having turned the hill-top, are on our way down to the grave. It is a solemn position that culminating point, where we see the cradle we have left on this side, and the grave where we shall lie on that! Yet it is not of much practical consequence to know whether we are going up or down hill, since there are in disease and the chapter of accidents many causes which make it the lot of few to number the appointed threescore years and ten. Death strikes down his victims at all ages; and of the crowd that started together, but two or three stragglers reach the natural term of life. Many more die young than old: and death so extends his ravages over the whole period of life, that, whether with buoyant steps we are pressing up or are tottering down hill beneath a load of years, we tread on graves; the road, if I may say so, is paved with burial stones; and on every side the tombs of all ages, each with its *memento mori*, tell the young not less than the old to prepare to die.

> " Leaves have their time to fall,
>   And flowers to wither at the north wind's breath;
>   And stars to set; but all—
>   Thou hast all seasons for thine own, O Death!"

Still, as where no river flows, or mountains rise to divide one kingdom from another, though the border land between life's growth and decay is not often very clearly marked, our Maker, for wise and kind ends, has given very distinct and distinguishing features to infancy, to youth, to manhood, and to old age. Infancy, in which man of all creatures is most dependent on others, requires constant help and care; besides needing these, old age, marked by its gray hairs, has sacred claims on our sympathies and respect. Nature herself teaches us to look with reverence on age, even in the pages of an old book; in the leafless branches of an old tree; in the silent, deserted halls of an old roofless ruin: still more in one whose head is white with the snows of fourscore or a hundred winters; still more in yon aged pilgrim who sits on Jordan's bank, straining his eyes to catch a glimpse of the shining ones that wait to welcome him beyond death's dark flood. "The hoary head is a crown of glory, if it be found in the way of righteousness," as seen in Simeon in the temple, where, with Jesus held in arms that trembled with joy more than age, he bent his hoary head to gaze with awe, and affection, and adoration on the infant's face; and raised it to astonish the bystanders—admiring only in them the beautiful conjunction of age and infancy, of life's rosy dawn and evening gray—with this ardent, heavenly, this death-defying and death-desiring wish, Lord, now lettest thou thy servant depart in peace, according to thy word: for mine eyes have seen thy salvation.

Gray hairs, what tender authority do they add to the law, "Honour thy father and thy mother: that thy days may be long upon the land which the Lord thy God giveth thee!" I care nothing for the religion of man or woman who, neglecting aged and venerable parents, leaves them to the care of strangers; casting those on the cold charities of the world whom they should have protected and nourished, in return for the kindness that watched over their feeble years, and bore with the foibles and follies of their youth. Although the deserted, dying savage, beating the withered breasts at which a son drank in life, has complained of him who forgot even in the pressure of sorest want a mother's kindness and a mother's claims, yet for those wandering tribes that, pressed by hunger, and ever on the verge of famine, feel the old men who cannot hunt and the old women who cannot walk to be burdens, and throw them off, there is some excuse; but for those of us who neglect the claims of parents—none. In such men's profession there is no reality or truth. He who does not revere a father he has seen, cannot love a Father whom he has not seen.

Other gray hairs besides those of parents have claims on our respect. "Thou shalt rise up before the hoary head, and honour the face of the old man," is a command that speaks to our hearts, and is in harmony with the best feelings of our nature. Nor in public assembly have I ever seen a feeble old man, bending under the weight of years, or, perhaps, of sorrow, left standing, while stout youth and manhood sat lounging at ease, but the spectacle has recalled the words of that noble Greek who, seeing an aged man left to stand a butt for youths to jeer at, rose in indignation to rebuke the crime, and tell his degenerate countrymen how, in the better days of the republic, on an old man entering an assembly all rose to their feet to do him reverence. Gray hairs mark the decay of man; but contempt for gray hairs, and want of respect in children to parents, or in youth to age, is a sign that virtue, society, and the Church of God decay. There is no worse or more evil-omened feature in American society than the forwardness and pretensions of its youth; nor, for we have our own faults, is there a greater social evil in this old country than the growing indifference that children shew to the feelings or comfort of their aged parents. To cast them, without strong necessity, on public charity, however agreeable it may be to law, is contrary to nature, to the dictates of the gospel, and to the blessed example of him who from his dying cross cast looks of love on Mary, and committed her with most touching tenderness to the care of John.

In my text, however, gray hairs are not associated either with parental honours, or with the ripe wisdom of age, or with the piety of the venerable Simeon. They are here but the tokens of decay, marks of age, the premonitory symptoms of dissolution; and so the truth it announces is that men, many men, live in ignorance, and act in disregard of signs that should warn and alarm them.

In illustration of this, I remark—

1. It appears in the history of States.

These words were first spoken of the kingdom of Israel. In the oppression of the poor and the sighing of the needy, in the corruption of morals and the decline of true religon, the prophet saw the signs of his country's decay—these the gray hairs that were here and there upon them, and they knew not. Nor is that uncommon. Fell consumption wears roses on her cheek, nor parts with hope but with life; and kingdoms, as well as men and women in decline, stricken with a mortal malady, have descended into the grave, blind to their dangers and their doom. What an example of this the disruption of Rehoboam's kingdom! The dissolute habits of his father's court, with such a tendency as water has to seek a lower level, had extended to the community, and corrupted its morals; the palace, from which religion had been scared by the introduction of idolatry and strange women, had forfeited all claim to public respect; the crown, associated with open profligacy and the basest selfishness, had lost its brightest gems; the throne that David had left to his descendants, with none to rally round it but men enervated by luxury and debased by vice, was ready to fall at the first shock; while the people, restive under their burdens, were ripe for rebellion. Such were the circumstances in which, at Solomon's death, his son was called to the helm—breakers ahead; breakers on the lee bow; white roaring breakers on this side and on that! But the pilot was blind. When circumstances called for the most skilful seamanship, reckless, he ran his ship ashore; straight on ruin. Insensible to his dangers, he had not even the discretion to return a civil answer, a decent refusal, to his people's petitions; telling those who asked that their burdens might be made lighter, the yoke less grievous, "My little finger shall be thicker than my father's loins. And now whereas my father did lade you with a heavy yoke, I will add to your yoke: my father hath chastised you with whips, but I will chastise you with scorpions." What man ever so played the fool on a royal stage, or more plainly illustrated the words of the heathen moralist —The gods first make mad those whom they intend to destroy? Such was his answer. The result was not long to wait for. In less than four and twenty hours the country was in arms; what, well guided, had resulted in reform, exploded in a revolution which hurled this madman from the throne of Israel, and left him but a fragment of his father's kingdom. Gray hairs were here and there upon him, and yet he knew not.

May his fate be our warning! We boast of our wealth; that our commerce extends to every region; that our manufactories are the workshops of the world; that our armies have pushed their conquests to the ends of the earth; that our Queen rules an empire on which the sun never sets; that the slave who touches our shore is free, and the beaten patriot who flies to its refuge is safe; how, beneath the ægis of Liberty, Peace sits crowned, while Plenty pours a full horn into her lap; and best of all, how the Bible is open, and its preaching free; and that religion, while it commands the respect of all, is enthroned in the hearts and rules the lives of many. We think that our mountain stands strong; and that we are as safe amid the revolutions that shake other countries as this island, guarded by its rocky cliffs, amid the storms that agitate the sea. I am not sure of that; there are gray hairs on us. What do you say to an amount of illegitimacy that disgraces our Christian name, and calls on masters and parents to guard the virtue of their homes? What say you to the drunkenness which costs us, year by year, vast millions of money and whole hecatombs of human lives? What do you say to the loose morality which, imported from the Continent, is fast destroying the claims which the upper classes of society have on the respect of the lower? What to the altars that stand in ruins in so many households, to the multitudes that take their pleasure on God's holy day, and to the audacious attempts made to turn our Sabbaths into days of worldly pleasure? What to the thousands in our large, the tens of thousands in our larger, and the hundreds of thousands in our largest cities, that have thrown off the profession of religion, and from year's end to year's end never enter a house of God? In these I see gray hairs, signs of national decay; nor could I, but for one thing, anticipate any other fate for our country than that which has entombed Egypt and Assyria, Babylon and Persia, Greece and Rome— first birth, then growth, then decay, then death, then the grave. With gray hairs here and there on us, we do know it. Thank God, we know it; and that thousands of earnest men and devoted women, fired with love to God and souls, animated by piety and the truest patriotism, are alive to our evils and working hard to cure them. There is balm in Gilead and a physician there; and though I do not know that hair once gray ever turns black again, our country, like an eagle, may renew its youth, and mounting as on eagle's wings, rise higher and higher still. To America, could my voice reach her shores, or be heard above the rage of passions and the roar of battle, and to our own country also I would address the words of the prophet: If thou take away from the midst of thee the yoke, the putting forth of the finger, and speaking vanity; and if thou draw out thy soul to the hungry, and satisfy the afflicted soul, then shall thy light rise in obscurity, and thy darkness shall be as the noonday; and the Lord shall guide thee continually, and satisfy thy soul in drought, and make fat thy bones; and thou shalt be like a watered garden, and like a spring of water, whose waters fail not.

2. My text applies to the false security of sinners.

It is a dreadful thing to see the happiness of a human being, like a brittle vase, shattered at a blow; the fair fabric collapse in an instant into a heap of ruins. It is more painful still to have to strike the blow. With reluctant steps I have approached the house of a young wife to communicate tidings of her husband's death. There is not a cloud in that summer's sky; nor, as she thinks, in hers. The air rings with songs of happy birds, and the garden amid which her home stands is full of smiling beauty; and fair as the flowers and happy as a singing bird comes that bride forth, rushing out to bid me welcome to her sunny home. With such tidings I felt like an executioner. I thought of victims going with garlands to the sacrifice. With Jephthah, when his child came forth with dances and delight to meet him, I was ready to cry, " Alas! my daughter;" and when the truth was told, the knife plunged into her heart, and she, springing to her feet, with one wild, long, piercing shriek, dropped on the floor at mine, a senseless form, I felt it hard to have such offices to do. I could not give her back her dead, nor at her wild entreaties unsay the dreadful truth, or admit, poor soul! that I was but playing with her fears. But how happy would I esteem myself to break in on your false security? Here to dream is death, but to wake is life; as yonder, when you break in on the baseless visions of a prison, and shewing an open door to the felon who has woke to the miserable consciousness of his doom, bid him rise and flee—saying, Behold, I have set before thee an open door! But, perhaps, you have no fears, at least are not much alarmed; counting yourselves rather certain than otherwise of escaping hell and finding heaven at death. On what grounds, may I ask? Have you been converted? Is Christ precious to you? Have you washed in the fountain of his blood? Have you waited at the gates of prayer? Have you made your calling and election sure? Have you the witness of God's Spirit and the testimony of your conscience within you, that in simplicity and godly sincerity you have your conversation in the world? No: then be assured that gray hairs are upon you, the greatest dangers beset you, and, alas, you know not.

Frequenting the church, repairing so many times a year to the Lord's table, assembling once a day, or perhaps oftener, your household to prayers, you make a becoming profession. There were more hope of some if they did not. Harlots and publicans who feel that they have nothing, and none but Christ to trust to, press into the kingdom, leaving scribes and Pharisees at the back of the door. A plausible profession, like false hair worn to hide the gray, may but conceal the signs of our danger. Take away from some their profession, and what remains? The outside religion subtracted, nothing; or only what might suggest the unwrapping of yon tenant of a dusty tomb on the banks of the Nile. Once it was a man or lovely woman; but now, these painted, odorous, gilded cerements, fold by fold, removed, we reach a blackened mummy—a withered skeleton. Hidden from view by a fair profession, the world, the devil, hideous and unholy passions lodge within the heart, where God and Christ should be.

Be our profession what it may, if we have habits of sin—these are the gray hairs that, unless grace convert and mercy pardon, foretell our doom. Thick as these on the head of age, some men's lives are full of sin; they are going to hell as plainly as one whose form is bent and whose head is hoary is going down to his grave. But you may have abandoned many sins! Ah, but what is this? Here is a sin, small indeed, and secret, and unknown to the world, of which no man even suspects you; yet, like the one gray hair among her golden or raven tresses, which the vain beauty sees with dismay, it points to the grave. Oh, trust to no Saviour but Christ, nor to any evidence of a gracious state other than an entire abstinence from all sin; or, at least, godly sorrow for it, and daily resistance to it! So long as you see one star in the sky, the sun is not risen; so long as one leak admits the water, the ship is not safe; so long as one sin reigns in a man's heart, and is practised in his life, Jesus is neither his Saviour nor his King. The Jews have no dealings with the Samaritans.

3. This appears in men's insensibility to the lapse and lessons of time.

It is one of the most beautiful and beneficent arrangements of Providence, that children, if sensible of their helplessness, are not ashamed of that which awakens our love and sympathy; it gives them no pain. Nor less kind on God's part is it that our minds are formed to adapt themselves to the circumstances of advancing years. Indeed we often glide so gently, so gradually down the decline of life, as to be little disturbed with the premonitions of its close. I remember the saying of a venerable lady, who had seen the changes of fourscore summers: "Let no one trust to this, that they will turn to God, and seek a Saviour when they feel old; I don't feel old." And though the young perhaps will hardly credit it, men with furrows in their brow, and gray hairs on their head, often find it difficult to remember that they are old; to believe it; to realise the approach of their end; how near they are to the grave. Death seems to flee before us, like the horizon which we ever see, and never reach. The river that springs like an arrow from its rocky cradle, to bound from crag to crag, to rush brawling through the glen, and, like thoughtless youth, to waste its strength in mere noise, and froth, and foam, flows on smoothly, slowly, almost imperceptibly, as it approaches its grave in the bosom of the sea. And so is it often with man. The nearer we draw to our end, through a natural callousness or otherwise, the less sensible we grow to the evils and approach of age. And when a man has not left his peace with God to seek in old age, his greatest work to a time when he is least fit to do it; when a man, having made his calling and election sure, has left nothing for a dying hour but to enjoy the comforts and peace of piety; in such a case it is a most blessed thing that old age does not make our hearts old, or benumb our feelings—that gray hairs are on us, and yet we know not.

But where, in such a case, is the hope of those who have trusted to turning religious when they turn old, and attending to the concerns of a better world when they have ceased to feel any interest in this? Death and a man, so runs the story, once made a bargain—the man stipulating, lest he might be taken unawares, that Death should send him so many warnings before he came. Well, one day, years thereafter, to his great amazement, the King of Terrors stood before him. He had broken the bargain, so said the other, who clung to life. Death, he alleged, had sent him no warnings. No warnings? His eyes were dim; his ears were dull; his gums were toothless; and spare and thin were the hoar locks on his bent and palsied head; these, Death's heralds, had come, not too late, yet all in vain. Amid warnings, but unnoticed or despised, his salvation was neglected; his soul lost; gray hairs were on him; and, so far as any practical effect was concerned, he knew not. Literally, or not, they are on us. Every setting sun, and every nodding hearse, and every passing Sabbath, warn us that days of darkness come, and opportunities of salvation go. Be up, therefore, and doing—asking yourselves such questions as these: Am I saved? Have I been born again? Have I embraced the Saviour? If not, oh, seize this flying hour!

He taught a solemn truth who painted Time as an old man, with wings on his shoulders, scythe and hour-glass in his hands, and on his wrinkled forehead one lock of hair. All bald behind, and offering us no hold when it is past, let us seize Time by the forelock. Be saved this hour! That hoary preacher addresses you, as he shakes a glass where the sands of some of us are well-nigh run, and points his finger to the grave which, a few years hence, shall have closed over all this living assembly. Like other preachers, he shall die. Death himself shall die; but we never. Blessed or cursed with immortality, we shall live to wish we had never lived, or to rejoice that we shall live for ever. And, whether they fall late or early, happy then and happy now, such as, not ignorant that there were gray hairs on them, guilt in their lives, and sins on their consciences, sought salvation in Jesus Christ—washing their stains away in that atoning blood which both cleanseth from the vilest sins, and is free to the worst of sinners!

II.

FEAR, THE FRUIT OF DIVINE FORGIVENESS.

"There is forgiveness with thee, that thou mayest be feared."—
PSALM CXXX. 4.

WERE we told that the worm that crawls, wriggling across our path, would one day rise a winged form to soar aloft and glitter in the sunny air like a living gem; were we told that a dry, husky, sapless, dead-like thing, if buried, would spring from its grave, changed in colour and form, to become a flower of fairest hues, or a tree with tough timbers to form the ribs, or tall stem the mast of a mighty ship; were we told that water may be made as hard as stone, or that, before the smoke of its last gun has melted into air, the news of a battle may be borne hundreds of miles away, along an iron wire, through the bowels of mountains, or over the bed of the sea; which of us, if previously ignorant of them, would not be filled with wonder, if not with incredulity? We meet much to startle us, much that is unlikely, unexpected in the works of God. No wonder, therefore, that we should stumble on passages to startle us here and there in his Word; statements of duty, of fact, of doctrine, to surprise us, and prompt the exclamation of Nicodemus, when, hearing from our Saviour that man must be born again, he exclaimed, How can these things be?

Take, for example, such duties as these: "Whosoever shall smite thee on thy right cheek, turn to him the other also. And if any man will sue thee at the law, and take away thy coat, let him have thy cloak also." "If thine enemy hunger, feed him; if he thirst, give him drink." "Love your enemies, bless them that curse you, do good to them that hate you, and pray for them which despitefully use you, and persecute you." How natural for men, ignorant of the power of grace, as some are of those powers in nature that change a creeping worm into a winged insect, or water which a breath can ruffle into a pavement as solid as stone, and deeming such heights of virtue impossible, to exclaim with the Jewish ruler, How can these things be? So also might they have said, who listened with astonishment to the opening sentences of our Lord's first and of the world's greatest sermon—"Blessed are the poor in spirit," "Blessed are they that mourn," "Blessed are the meek," "Blessed are ye when men shall revile you and persecute you, and shall say all manner of evil against you falsely for my sake." This was a flight as high above the style of common preachers as that of the eagle disturbed in her mountain solitudes, and, at that moment, soaring in the blue heavens above their heads. Accustomed to shrink from poverty in every form, from loss and grief, from persecution and calumny, as evils to be avoided, I can fancy the people casting on each other looks of surprise, doubt, and amazement, which said, as plainly as spoken words, How can these things be?

Then there are doctrinal statements in the Word of God where the two parts of the sentence do not seem to hang well together. For example, "Hearken unto me, ye stout-hearted, that are far from righteousness." God here brings a charge of guilt against his people; and how does he wind up the sentence? Imagine a trial for murder, for instance! Arrayed in his robes of office, the judge, amid solemn silence, receives their verdict from the jury. It is, Guilty. And in what terms does he now address the pale, wretched, trembling felon at the bar! Fixing on him eyes full at once of pity and of horror, he says, You have been charged with the crime of murder, and, after a fair, full, patient trial, have been found guilty; and now the sentence of the law is, that you be taken back to prison, and from prison to the place of execution, and there be hanged by the neck till you are dead. Where man begins with a conviction, he ends with condemnation; a judgment of guilt is followed up by a sentence of death. Not so God in this case. Hearken unto me, ye stout-hearted, ye guilty, bold, bad, daring sinners, that are far from righteousness—what follows? Not, I will beat your stout-heartedness out of you, breaking you with a rod of iron, dashing you in pieces like a potter's vessel; but, "I bring near my righteousness." Had this address—calling up the pictures of the prodigal kneeling at his father's feet, of Peter without, weeping bitterly and filling the ear of night with long-drawn sobs, of the woman washing Christ's feet with tears, and wiping them with her golden tresses—begun differently; had it begun thus, Hearken unto me, ye bleeding, broken-hearted ones, that are far from righteousness, I bring near mine, its conclusion had been less surprising. But it is as if a great, black, lurid, leaden cloud, on which we have been gazing with silent dread, expecting it each moment to burst in thunders, were to dissolve itself in a shower which cools the sultry air, and refreshes the thirsty ground.

Such another example of apparent incongruity is afforded by the first and second members of the text, "There is forgiveness with thee, that thou mayest be feared!" That thou mayest be feared! we are ready to ask, How does that follow? How can these things be? There is forgiveness with thee! a blessed truth that! one we gladly assent to; nay, hail, as the Israelites, on that night when the sea roared in their front and Egypt pressed on their rear, hailed the path which, stretching from shore to shore, opened them a way of escape. But for that they must have all been drowned; but for this we must have all been damned—for were God to mark iniquity, or enter into judgment, who could stand? who could answer for one of a thousand?

In opening up the subject of my text I observe,

I. That there must be something peculiar about God's forgiveness that it leads to fear.

"Honour thy father and thy mother," says the law, "that thy days may be long upon the land which the Lord thy God giveth thee." But how can this be done when parents, ever threatening, and hardly ever punishing, set their children an example of weakness, if not of wickedness? "Foolishness is bound in the heart of a child," and must be separated from it by beating, as the husk from the grain ere it is fit for the oven, or the woody fibre from the flax ere it is fit for the loom. Hence Solomon says, He that spareth his rod hateth his son. It is the forked lightning which, leaping from the clouds with a roar, rends the stoutest oak, men dread; not the sheet lightning, which, though startling us at first as it glares on the darkness of night, we have learned to regard with indifference. It shines, but does not strike; it flashes, but does not fall. No parents are less revered by their children than those who deal in empty threats, and reverse, if I may say so, the exclamation of Isaac, The voice is Jacob's voice, but the hands are the hands of Esau. So to threaten and not to punish is about as fatal to the well-being of a family, as to promise and not reward. An act of forgiveness following on every offence slacks the bonds of obedience; and a constant repetition of acts of forgiveness on the part of a weak parent, encourages a constant repetition of acts of offence on the part of a wicked child. By and by the hand that has sown the wind reaps the whirlwind. Disobedience in the child grows into a habit; its nature becomes thoroughly perverted; its regard for parental authority dies; and in the indulgent parents, whose gray hairs their children treat with contempt and probably bring with sorrow to the grave, in the wretchedness of their homes and the utter wreck of their families, we have an illustration of this grand law of domestic life, that where parents will not punish their children, their children, the least guilty party and most sinned against, will punish them. There must, therefore, be a very essential difference between the forgiveness of our heavenly and that of many an earthly father, else were these words not true, "There is forgiveness with thee, that thou mayest be feared."

Had my text run thus, There is power, justice, anger, vengeance with thee; or, in accordance with such statements as these, "Cursed is every one that continueth not in all things which are written in the book of the law to do them," "The soul that sinneth, it shall die;" had my text said, There is truth with thee, who would not have seen this to be the plain, natural, solemn conclusion, "that thou mayest be feared!" Let God arm himself with terrors, and we feel that he is to be feared.

On the deep, where giant billows, rushing on with foaming crest, threaten instant destruction; beneath the lurid sky when, bursting in thunder peals, every bolt threatens instant death; when the pestilence, wrapped in folds of poisonous vapours, walks the streets of an alarmed city, and funerals are met at every turn, and friends and neighbours seized in the darkness of the night are dead before morning, stubborn knees bend in prayer, and terror sits on the faces of stout-hearted men; ah, then "the perpetual hills did bow, ... the mountains saw thee, and they trembled;" or in the words of another prophet, "The lion hath roared, who will not fear?" And so, had my text in connexion with God introduced scenes of terror — the great white throne; the books of judgment; the falling heavens; the dying sun; the departing earth; the pit; the smoke of torment; the worm that never dies, and the fire that is never quenched; the solemn scene that shall wind up the close of all things, a God in judgment, and a world in flames—all hearts would have responded like an echo, to the text, and this question had trembled on our lips, "Who shall not fear thee, O Lord, and glorify thy name? for thou only art holy."

But this is not the way. And how is it, that while the parents who constantly forgive are not feared, God, with whom is forgiveness, is? why is it that forgiveness does not in his case, as in theirs, breed insolent presumption? What is that strange and potent element in divine forgiveness which makes the forgiven fear—making me more afraid to sin beside the Cross of Calvary, with its quiet, pale, dead, bleeding burden, than if I stood at the foot of Sinai amid the thunders, lightnings, and trumpet peals that made Moses himself exceedingly fear and quake? In other words, how is it that, because there is not power, nor judgment, nor terror, but forgiveness with God, he is therefore to be feared, and is feared?

II. Let me explain those peculiar characters in the forgiveness of God which breed fear, not presumption, in the forgiven.

1. The manner of the forgiveness sets forth the holiness of God and the evils of sin in the strongest light.

The heathen have little fear of their gods. How should they fear them? They can make a god out of a piece of wood, or buy one for a shilling. With how little reverence some treat their divinities is related by a missionary who saw what he relates with his own eyes. The country had been suffering from long and severe drought; and unless rain came, the fields must wither, and the people die of famine. Prayer was made to their gods, with whom their worshippers, having received no answer, got very angry; and as I have seen a child beat the table on which, falling, he had hurt his head, or with little hands beat the nurse who, refusing some request, had crossed his temper, the missionary saw these simple, ignorant, blinded pagans drag their idols from the temple, and, pouring on their heads a torrent of reproaches, whip them soundly. And when we turn from such rude barbarians to the polished heathens of Greece and Rome, how little reverence did they entertain for their gods! and, though possessing a code of moral laws in some respects not much inferior to our own, how did the great mass of them live impure and unholy, in flagrant violation of all morality! Observant of the ceremonial parts of their religion, they allowed its moral laws to be no check on their vices. By the masses these laws were openly, systematically, and shamelessly violated. It is so still among heathens, who, though pagans, are not barbarians—among, for example, both the Buddhists and Hindoos of the East. Read the moral precepts of Buddha, and you will be astonished at their purity. Their correspondence with our own ten commandments, which is as startling as it is pleasing, presents a most remarkable illustration of the fact that the law which God wrote on the granite tables of Sinai was a copy of the old law that he had written on the fleshy tables of man's heart, where you may still trace the original writing, like the mutilated inscription on a shattered and weathered stone. Yet what effect have these admirable laws on the habits of the people? None, or almost none, in restraining them from the practice of the grossest vices; exerting as little influence on their lives as do the stars on our destinies.

How do we account for these facts? Nothing

more easy. These nations, like ourselves, believe in a future state and a judgment to come; their world beyond the grave, no less than ours, has its heaven and hell; and human fancy, under an awakened and alarmed conscience, has pictured nothing more dreadful than the punishments of their Tartarus, the torments of their damned. But what blunts the edge of all this, neutralising its power over their hearts, and making it practically of little, or rather of no avail, is the fact that, according to their creed, sin is forgiven on very easy terms. That is the dead fly in all systems of salvation by works. Pagan or popish, they are immoral in their tendency. This explains why those who have been most taught to seek salvation through good works have been least distinguished for the practice of them; and why the more these, substituted for the Cross, have been preached on the Sabbath-day, the less they have been practised throughout the week. For, to return to the case of the heathen, how could they think sin to be exceedingly sinful, or, holding their gods in reverence, fear to offend them, when, according to the terms on which forgiveness was granted, it was safer to offend God than men?—man requiring his debtor to pay the uttermost farthing, but God requiring of one who sought to escape the wrath and curse due to him for sin, only some words of prayers, or the performance of a religious ceremony, or the blood of some brute creature. The natural, logical, inevitable conclusion which men drew from such views was, that the gods attached little importance to their own laws, else they would not be so easily appeased by the transgressors of them. There was forgiveness with them, but it was not of a kind to deter their worshippers from sin—filling their hearts with godly fear.

Turn now to the cross of Calvary, to that august and awful spectacle on which angels, suspending their songs, are gazing in silent wonder. By that bloody tree, under that frowning sky, the earth trembling beneath our feet and the sun darkened above our heads, does sin seem a light and little thing? In God's words to Ezekiel, while I point to that cross, I ask, "Hast thou seen this, O son of man? Is it a light thing to the house of Judah that they commit the abominations which they commit here?" A little thing? Sin a little thing? You think so; and you are right, if, as my breath blows out a candle, or a drop of water quenches it, a prayer, a penitent sigh, or a few dropping tears can extinguish the wrath of God. It is so, if the mere expression of our sorrow, a slight repentance, can pay our debts to God, though, as you know well, they would be accepted as payment of them by no one else. It is so, if that blinded Papist, who embraces a life of poverty, who leaves a pillow of down for a bed on the cold ground, who wears a shirt of sackcloth, who, summoned by the convent bell, rises at midnight to prayer, or, fleeing the haunts of men, seeks the desert and the society of beasts, can, by such self-denial, make atonement to God for the sins of his soul. Great as his sufferings may be, an eternity of happiness is cheaply purchased by a whole lifetime of pain—as a lifetime of pleasure is certainly a dear bargain if enjoyed at the expense of eternal pains. But if, ere one sin could be pardoned or one sinner saved, heaven must give up the Lord of Glory, and the Son of God must die; if justice accepts no cheaper sacrifice; if "there is none other name under heaven given among men whereby we must be saved but the name," nor other blood whereby we can be washed but the blood of Jesus, sin is no light and little thing.

"Wherewith," asks the prophet, "shall I come before the Lord, and bow myself before the high God? Will the Lord be pleased with thousands of rams, or with ten thousands of rivers of oil?" Thousands of rams! The smoke of such a sacrifice ascending to the skies, and rolling its murky clouds over the face of heaven, might blot out the sun; but it hides not the smallest sin from the keen eyes of God. Ten thousands of rivers of oil! Pour them on the stormy sea when our bark is battling for life, and they lay its roughest waves; but it needs the form and feet, the presence and the voice of our Redeemer, to turn the storm within my soul into a calm, and say to a troubled conscience, Peace, be still. But the prophet speaks of a sacrifice more costly than flocks of rams or rivers of oil. "Shall I give my first-born for my transgression, the fruit of my body for the sin of my soul?" Well, fancy *that* the price demanded by God for sin, and that you see a father about to pay it. With downcast head, and slow, reluctant steps, he approaches the altar where his first-born lies, ready bound. You see him kneel to embrace and kiss his boy; to beg delay; to pray the stern heavens for pity or for strength to do this stern duty. He rises, and while the mother in anguish covers her eyes, he slowly bares the steel and raises his arm to strike; and when your sight grows dim, your ears catch a dull stroke and a deep groan, followed by a gush of blood; now, as you fly a scene where the father lies fallen, fainting, on the bloody corpse, were such the price God required for sin, how would you exclaim, It is not a light and little thing to sin against the Lord—Great is the Lord, and greatly to be praised: he also is to be feared above all gods—Holy, holy, holy, is the Lord of hosts!

It is by an altar and through a victim that there is forgiveness with God; pardon flows to men in a stream of blood. But here the altar is a cross, and its victim is the Son of the Highest. "Hast thou seen this, O son of man?"—God incarnate hung between two thieves; the Author of all life yielding up his own; the conqueror of death dying; the feet that walked the billows, the hands that raised the dead and burst the fetters of the tomb, nailed to a bloody tree—for thee —all for thee—that thou mightest be forgiven? With his dying eyes fixed on you, within sound of his dying groans, and of that cry that startled the heavens, My God, my God, why hast thou forsaken me? does not sin, only to be atoned for by so great a sacrifice, appear exceeding sinful? There is forgiveness, but after a fashion that should teach us to fear, and, in life's lightest hours, to join trembling with our mirth. Our pardon is written in letters of blood; the hand that bestows the crown bears the marks of a cross; it is a wounded form, a "Lamb as it had been slain," that fills the throne of the universe. Looking at these things, "Who shall not fear thee, O Lord?" If such things were done in the green tree, oh! what shall be done in the dry? If God did not spare his only-begotten and well-beloved Son when he took our sins on him, how shall he spare those who prefer their sins to their Saviour—neglecting this great salvation?

2. The manner of forgiveness sets forth not only God's hatred of sin, but his love to sinners in the strongest light.

Parents are often moved to forgive, or at least not to punish, their children from selfish motives, overlooking the offences not so much because they love their children as that they love themselves—themselves better than their children. Of a tender and sensitive nature, the parent in punishing often feels more acutely than the child who is punished; the strokes that fall on its flesh fall on his bleeding heart.

And it inflicts such distress on many to see the tears standing in a child's eye and to hear its cries, that they, to escape this pain, allow their children to go unpunished; and since, in Solomon's judgment, this is practically to hate the child, how much did we owe those who, having, in the days of their flesh, not for their own pleasure, but with much self-inflicted pain, corrected us for our good, have left us to regret that when we had them we did not prize them more and pay them greater reverence! It may be no proof of parental love for a parent to forgive.

Besides, to forgive man in any circumstances costs us nothing. Say that he has defrauded me; injured my reputation; attempted my life; and suppose such an enemy in my power; what does it cost me to forgive him? Let us see. To reduce him to poverty would make me no richer; to destroy his peace would not restore my own; to hurt him would not heal me; to break his heart would not bind up mine; to cast a blot on his reputation would restore no lustre to my name; to take his life, saying with the bloody Papist and persecutor of God's saints in France, "Nothing smells so sweet as the dead body of an enemy," would not insure me against the stroke of death, nor lengthen my life by a single hour. It is no great proof of love after all for you or me to forget an injury and forgive the injurer. To pardon a criminal may smooth the cares and soothe the sorrows of a royal pillow, but adds none to them; it may augment but cannot diminish the lustre of a crown. It is a happy memory that remembers kindness, and forgets offences. It is a far nobler thing to conquer one's passions than to crush a foe; and sweeter than gratified revenge are his feelings who, when his enemy hungers, feeds him; when he thirsts, gives him drink. In so doing, man exhibits somewhat of the nature, and tastes something of the happiness, of God.

From the forgiveness of man turn to that of God. It is hard to say whether it most illustrates his hatred of our sins or his love of ourselves. It costs man nothing to forgive, but it cost God his Son. His Son? How painful it is to look on a dying son— even a dying infant; to watch life's sad and solemn ebbings; to see the last quiver of the little lips; to lay the pale, cold, dead body we have so often carried in our happy arms, in the coffin and the cold grave? I dare not say that God bent over his dying Son with feelings corresponding to ours; that he hung over the cross as we have hung over the cradle; or that the strange perturbations in nature, a trembling earth and rending rocks, heavens palled in darkness, and the sun turned pale with terror, though they may perhaps have extended to worlds beyond our own, reached up to the throne of nature's God. I cannot fathom, and I dare not fancy the feelings of the eternal Father, when he saw the Son whom he loved with infinite affection spit upon, scourged, reviled, bleeding, dying on the accursed tree. But how must he have loved you for whom he gave a Son so loved? and how will the love this breeds in you make you fear to dishonour or displease one who has so loved you—securing your forgiveness on such an immovable foundation and at so great a price.

To believe yourselves forgiven, while you love sin and live in the practice of it, is to believe a lie—a monstrous lie. Whom God justifies he sanctifies, and the sense of forgiveness which is inwrought by his Holy Spirit, cannot fail to produce holy fears and strenuous efforts after new obedience—such an effect as resulted in a case which not inaptly illustrates both the way in which God deals with sinners, and the obedience that springs from a sense of forgiveness. A soldier, whose regiment lay in a garrison town in England, was about to be brought before his commanding officer for some offence. He was an old offender, and had been often punished. Here he is again, said the officer, on his name being mentioned; everything —flogging, disgrace, imprisonment—has been tried with him. Whereupon the serjeant stepped forward, and apologising for the liberty he took, said, There is one thing which has never been done with him yet, sir. What is that? was the answer. Well, sir, said the serjeant, he has never been forgiven. Forgiven! exclaimed the colonel, surprised at the suggestion. He reflected for a few minutes, ordered the culprit to be brought in, and asked him what he had to say to the charge? Nothing, sir, was his reply; only

I am sorry for what I have done. Turning a kind and pitiful look on the man, who expected nothing else than that his punishment would be increased with the repetition of his offence, the colonel addressed him, saying, Well, we have resolved to forgive you! The soldier was struck dumb with astonishment; the tears started in his eyes, and he wept like a child. He was humbled to the dust, he thanked his officer and retired —to be the old, refractory, incorrigible man? No; he was another man from that day forward. He who tells the story had him for years under his eye, and a better conducted man never wore the Queen's colours. In him kindness bent one whom harshness could not break; he was conquered by mercy, and, forgiven, ever afterwards feared to offend. Shall the goodness and grace of God have less effect on us? Shall we continue in sin, that grace may abound? God forbid. Let the forgiven fear; and, oh, let none offered a greater forgiveness, a pardon which cost God his Son, refuse so great a boon! Weigh well, I pray you, these solemn words, He that despised Moses' law died without mercy under two or three witnesses; of how much sorer punishment, suppose ye, shall he be thought worthy, who hath trodden under foot the Son of God, and hath counted the blood of the Covenant, wherewith he was sanctified, an unholy thing, and hath done despite unto the Spirit of grace?

III.

THE UNDECAYING POWER AND GRACE OF GOD.

" Behold, the Lord's hand is not shortened, that it cannot save; neither his ear heavy, that it cannot hear."—ISA. lix. I.

THE face of nature never seems to change. The strongest arm grows old and feeble; raven locks turn gray; wrinkles deform the finest face; the once graceful form bends tottering to the grave; and the mind itself not unfrequently seems to partake in the general decay, as if this immortal spirit were to perish with its mortal tenement. But the years which work such change on us roll over our world, like successive waves over a rock, leaving no trace behind. Each returning spring is welcomed with songs; every summer decks our meadows and gardens with the old flowers; and, as if her powers could suffer no decay, in crops of fruit and in fields of golden corn autumn year by year renews the bounties of Nature.

We revisit our birth-place after an absence, say of fifty years; and finding, with the exception of a few in whose wrinkled and withered faces we begin to recognise some features of our old, noisy, rosy, laughing companions, all our friends dead and gone, new faces in the school, a new tenant in every farm, a new peasant in every cottage, a new minister in every pulpit, and a new congregation in the pews, we might almost doubt whether we had been there before. But when we turn to look on nature, we might fancy that we had never left home, and that the last fifty years were nothing but a dream. The sun rises over the same hill, the moonbeams glitter on the same lake, the skies resound with the same songs, moorland and mountain are clad in the same flowery verdure, and the gray rocks look down as of old on the stream, that, as it winds its way, snake-like, through the valley, here brawls over the same stones, and there sweeps into the same swirling pool. And so is it everywhere with nature! The Pharaohs sleep in their stony sepulchres, and Moses in his lone mountain grave, but the Nile rolls on as in the day when the Hebrew mother committed her child to its waters, and to the providence of her God. David's harp is broken, and his skilful hand is dust, but the snows of Salmon shine as white as when he sang their praises; Kedron runs murmuring through the valley of Jehoshaphat as on the night our Saviour waded it to enter on his agony in the garden; Capernaum, Chorazin, Bethsaida! the place that once knew them knows them now no more; but the mountains of Galilee stand around her lake as they presented themselves to Jesus' eye. There we gaze on the very scenes which were familiar to him; we tread the very shores along which he often walked in lone and lofty meditation; we look on the very waters that bore up his blessed feet; and yonder, where a boat battles with the storm, and men are pulling for their lives, we might almost fancy we should see his form rise, and, by a word or wave of his hand, turn that tumbling sea into a scene of calm repose.

Yet, fixed as nature seems to be, on examining the matter more closely, we find there is nothing fixed: and that it is not her prerogative to say, "I change not." Change not! The snows of winter and the rains of summer are, however slowly, constantly altering the form and features of this great world; and by means of their ten thousand streams are carrying it off to its grave in the depths of ocean Nor is there in Alps or Andes a mountain that pierces the clouds with its snow-crowned head, which, to parody the words of Scripture, time may not thus address, What art thou, O great mountain? before my hand and power thou shalt become a plain. Change not! It is by constant, perpetual change that nature maintains that appearance of sameness which strikes us as so remarkable—just, to use a plain but expressive illustration, as it is by constant revolutions a spinning top keeps itself from falling. The fortunes of a Moses, a Joseph, an Esther, present no vicissitudes so sudden or remarkable as those which may be traced in an atom of matter. Loosed from the rock by the hand of the frost, swept by a mountain stream into the valley, and left by a flood on the bank, it enters into a blade of grass. Emblem of our mortality, the grass withers and dies, and feeding the heather by its decay, our atom next blooms in its purple bell. Cropped by the moor-cock, it is next whirring along the hill-side, when the eagle, stooping from the clouds, strikes down his prey, and our atom now rises in wings which cleave the sky. Death at length lays low this monarch of the air: falling from his cloudy realm, he dies; and, rotting on the soil, feeds the pastures where a lamb crops the flower into which our atom has passed. In time the lamb falls to the knife; and now, becoming the food of man, it enters into the hand that wields a sceptre; or curls in the tresses that lend grace to beauty; or speaks in the tongue that in the senate-house sways the councils of a nation, or from the pulpit invites sinners to the arms of the Saviour, and with proclamation of the mutability both of the heavens and earth, thus addresses the unchangeable Jehovah · Thou, Lord, in the beginning hast laid the foundation of the earth; and the heavens are the work of thine hands: they shall perish; but thou remainest; and they all shall wax old as doth a garment; and as a vesture shalt thou fold them up, and they shall be changed; but thou art the same, and thy years shall not fail.

On going forth by night, and fixing our attention on the heavenly bodies, we observe that every hour changes their position. The star that at its first appearance shone above our heads is now sinking in the west, while those we saw rise from the bosom of the deep, have climbed to the top of the sky—the whole host of heaven appears to be marching on, one orb only, the pole star, excepted. Around that they seem to roll, as the pivot on which the whole firmament turns. Bright guide of the mariner on the deep, in summer and winter nights, it alone appears to remain immovable, unchangeable, and unchanged. What it appears to be, God is. Among all beings animate and inanimate, of earth or heaven, there is but one in the universe fixed, immovable, unchangeable. He alone can say, "I am the Lord, I change not;" and therefore, speaking of him, the prophet says, "Behold, the Lord's hand is not shortened, that it cannot save; neither his ear heavy, that it cannot hear."

I. The case of the Jews, to whom these words were first addressed, does not shake our confidence in God's willingness or power to save.

I admit that the fortunes of that people do not at first sight appear to correspond with this very confident and comforting declaration. For where is Jerusalem? Where now is she that was once called "the joy of the whole earth," "the perfection of beauty," "the city of our God?" Insulting their captives, and persecuting instead of pitying those whom God had smitten, the men of Babylon bade the Hebrews take their harps from the willows, saying, Sing us one of the songs of Zion. It is base to hit a man when he is down; but were I to insult a Jew, the Bible would furnish me with keener sarcasm than the Babylonian's. Jerusalem's towers and palaces and temple have been devoured by fire; the very foundations of the city were turned up by the Roman's ploughshare; and the site of her holy sanctuary is at this day profaned by a Moslem mosque. She retains no vestige of her glory but some old colossal stones, beside which, like wall-flower clinging to a ruin, some poor Jews may be found weeping—kissing them with the affection that regards her very dust as dear. How taunting, insulting were it simply to repeat in their ears the words of that old, proud, patriotic psalm, Walk about Zion, and go round about her: tell the towers thereof. Mark ye well her bulwarks, consider her palaces, that ye may tell it to the generation following. What other answer theirs, but the touching, broken-hearted cry, Ichabod, the glory is departed! Yet on the day when the Roman legions beset her walls, the Lord's hand was not shortened, that it could not save; neither his ear heavy, that it could not hear. He heard the din of battle, he heard the roar of fire; and it was not because he could not, that he did not save.

And if we leave the ruins of Jerusalem to seek the Jews, where are they? One of their old prophets, looking along the vista of time, exclaims, A nation scattered and peeled! And into what countries have they not been scattered, and what country has not scattered and peeled them in return? For eighteen hundred years have they been fugitives and vagabonds; nor have their weary feet ever found a resting place on earth. Strange fate! For this they have to thank their fathers. They drank the water in which Pilate washed his hands—taking the guilt of Christ's murder on themselves. His blood, they cried, be on us, and on our children; blood this, the only blood, whose stain years never have effaced; nor will, till the time to favour Zion, the set time is come, when God will bring back his banished ones, and make good the promise: "I will bring them again into the land that I gave unto their fathers. Behold, I will send for many fishers, saith the Lord, and they shall fish them; and after will I send for many hunters, and they shall hunt them from every mountain, and from every hill, and out of the holes of the rocks." Till then, a church without a temple, a people without a country, a race without a home, a nation meted out and trodden down, they shall be a proverb and a by-word and a perpetual hissing.

Strange fortunes these! yet, far from proving God's hand to be shortened, they prove the very reverse. With the regularity of a law of nature, one of two fates has befallen all other conquered nations. Like the Indians of America, who have fallen before the white man, as their forests before his axe, they have been extirpated; or the conquered have intermarried with their conquerors to breed a race like ours, in whose veins flows the mingled tide of Roman, Celtic, Saxon, and Scandinavian blood. The fate of the Jews how different and how singular! They have been oppressed, persecuted, trodden under foot; and, like the grass which grows thickest when trodden on, they have thriven under oppression—bearing a charmed life—the true sons of their fathers in the land of Egypt; of whom it was said, the more they were afflicted, the more they multiplied and grew.

The Jews are everywhere—inhabiting every country, yet belonging to none; mixed with every people, but combining with none. By the thrones of kings, in the senate-house of nations, in the mart of business, in the ranks of armies, everywhere the same, the Jew preserves his nationality; his faith; his haughty pride; his blood so pure that, whether you encounter him in the streets of London, or Paris, or Rome, or Petersburg, or Pekin, you can tell at once by his features that he is a son of Abraham. They exist among others as no other race ever did—like oil in water; and like oil, too, where their talents and ambition have free play, they usually rise to the top. They are not a holy nation, nor are they zealous of good works; yet they are a peculiar people—a standing moral miracle; their history a mystery. Living, multiplying, flourishing amid circumstances that, by all the common laws of providence, should have been fatal to their existence, they illustrate my text—proving the unchanging and unchangeable power of God as plainly as Daniel safe among hungry lions, or the bush that burned, and, burning, was not consumed.

II. Consider the truths expressed by these words.

1. God's power to save is neither lost nor lessened.

Where there is a will there is a way. Applicable as that saying is to many cases where people could do what they pronounce impossible if they would only try, it is absolutely, universally true of none but God. What father and mother would not wish all their children to be saved, and that all should meet, none amissing, before the throne in glory? What pastor, worthy of a pulpit, does not wish all his people to be saved—every member of his flock gathered at last into the Good Shepherd's fold? But our power to help, to save, is not boundless. Limited by many circumstances, it often falls far short of our inclinations. So it was with that unhappy man whom the sinking wreck left in the roaring sea—with a child clinging to this arm, and its mother, his wife, to that. With his right hand free to buffet the billows, one he may bear to yon blessed shore, but not both. Encumbered, his strength fast failing, to save both is impossible; and now he must choose which to save. Dreadful alternative! He shakes off the child, and striking for the land, away from its dying cries, he leaves the creature that had clung to him to perish. It was for no such reason that Jesus bore to heaven one only of the thieves crucified by his side. True, but one was taken while the other was left; true, the wind bloweth where it listeth, and so is every one that is born of the Spirit; but that wretched man who perished by the cross, sinking into hell while he saw his fellow go soaring like a lark to heaven, was not lost because Christ's hand was shortened that it could not save; he was not, like that unhappy child, shaken off, though clinging to the Saviour and crying, Lord, save me, I perish. No, his loss finds its explanation in the key to the perdition of thousands who sit in churches and go to hell, in these sad, solemn, awful words, "Ye will not come to me, that ye might have life." Those only are excluded from heaven who exclude themselves.

Again, our power to help may not only fall short of our inclination, but, such as it is, may be lessened and impaired by years. What a striking illustration of this have we in David's history! He began and closed his battles by a personal encounter, a hand-to-hand fight, with the giant sons of Anak. But how great a change had the forty years of cares and griefs, of public toils and domestic trouble, that elapsed between these two battles, wrought on him who, lithe of limb, and fleet of foot, and quick of eye, and sure of aim, ran, sling in hand, to meet the boaster; and stopped his boasting, laying his head in the dust. At the last of his conflicts the old courage is there: the fire of youth blazes up from the ashes of age, but the strength is gone; gray locks fall from beneath his helmet; his eye, dim with years, has lost its eagle glance; no bursting away now like a deer-hound from the leash, to meet this other Philistine. They meet; and when sword strikes fire with sword, before the shower of blows that ring from the giant's arm on his casque, David is borne back; and but that Abishai threw himself before his king, one of Goliath's race had avenged Goliath's death, and plucked his greenest laurels from David's brow. His hand was shortened; and, more wise than he, the men of Israel, as they bore off their aged king and received on their shields the blows aimed at his old, gray head, said, Thou shalt go no more out with us to battle, that thou quench not the light of Israel.

Ah! the time comes when the actor must leave the public stage; when the reins drop from the leader's grasp; and the orator's tongue falters; and the workman's stout arm grows feeble; and the fire of wit is quenched; and the man of genius turns into a drivelling idiot; and men of understanding, without any second birth, pass into a second childhood. But the time shall never come when it can be said of Jesus, his hand is shortened, that it cannot save. No; "the same yesterday, and to-day, and for ever," there is nothing he ever did, in saving, blessing, sanctifying, that he cannot do again. This gives undying value to all the offers, invitations, and promises of the gospel. What he has done in other cases he can do in yours, closing wounds deep as Job's; healing backslidings bad as David's; receiving penitents vile as she who bathed his feet with tears; and saving sinners near to hell as he who found salvation on the very brink of death. I promise you the same pardon, grace, and mercy as that of which there is any record in the word of God. Christ's resources are inexhaustible; and here, therefore, one man's gain is no other man's loss. People fight for a place in the life-boat, because its accommodation is limited, but Christ has room for all. He is able to save to the uttermost. We cannot be too long or too great sinners to be saved; and my answer to any who, yielding to despair, say, Ah! it is impossible that we can be changed, is this, It is not impossible that you, but it is impossible that he can be changed. He cannot change or lie who said, " Him that cometh to me I will in no wise cast out."

2. The Lord's power to hear and answer prayer is neither lost nor lessened; his ear is not heavy, that it cannot hear.

On one occasion a party of our soldiers happened to enter a cottage that stood on ground which had been occupied by an enemy whom they were driving before them at the point of the bayonet An infant's cries attracted their attention, and they turned to look on a spectacle which, inured as they were to scenes of horror, woke their tenderest pity. A father's corpse lay stretched across the threshold where he had fallen, bravely fighting to protect those within; on the floor, amid a pool of blood, lay the mother, dead; and on her bosom an infant, all unconscious of its loss, wailed and cried as it sought to draw nourishment from her empty breast. Time was when its feeblest cry roused her from deepest slumbers; but there it cried, and there she lay unmoved,—her ear was heavy, that it could not hear. And had not God directed thither the steps of those brave men, and had not they, touched with pity, and gilding with so bright an example of humanity war's lurid clouds, wrapped up the creature tenderly, and borne it away through the smoke and fire of battle to be the child and care of their regiment, it had perished in a mother's arms, on a mother's bosom;—her hand was shortened, that it could not save. So perish none in Christ!

The saints of God are never in the circumstances of children on whose home death's darkest shadow lies, as, standing round his bed, they gaze with mingled grief, and fear, and awe, on a father's pallid face and lifeless form. The cause of their emotion, he lies himself unmoved; their cries pierce other ears, not his; their sorrows move others' pity, not his; their tears wake others' sympathy, not his; whatever betide them, now that the arm which won their bread has lost its power, they may starve, crying for food, and their mother has none to give them;—but his ear is heavy, that it cannot hear; his hand is shortened, that it cannot save. Our nearest and dearest earthly friends are but broken cisterns at the best. They are running low; day by day lower; and they one day shall be dry; but "the portion of Jacob is not like them." He hears the cries, the sighs, not the words only, but the wishes of his people; even the unuttered and unutterable sorrows of a broken heart.

This imparts undying value to all those instances of heard, accepted, answered, prayer of which the Bible is so full; answers common and miraculous, to prayers for blessings temporal and spiritual, in all variety of imaginable circumstances—prayer by saints and sinners; prayers offered with life's last breath and by childhood's lisping tongue; in royal palaces, and in loathsome dungeons; in a den of lions, and in the depths of ocean; for health in sickness, and for bread in famine; for patience under the sorest trials, and deliverance in the most hopeless circumstances; for pardon of the greatest sins, and mercy to the greatest sinners. Never was the Lord's hand shortened, that it could not save, nor his ear heavy, that it could not hear. Why, then, should you despond, far less despair? Did he save the thief when his own hands were nailed to the accursed tree? When dying himself, amid the agonies of the cross, with all God's billows and waves roaring over his own head, did he hear and heed the cry of that poor wretch sinking at his side?

> "'Tis finish'd—All his groans are past;
> His blood, his pain, and toils."

And now, exalted to the right hand of God, seated on

his Father's throne, with all power in earth and heaven, how confident may we be that he will hear the prayer of the destitute, and save them who are ready to perish! While the shadow of their crowns falls at our feet, the saints—among whom I see Job and Jonah, Moses and David, the man who was a thief, and the woman who was a sinner—bend from their celestial thrones to hold up the arms of prayer. Hear what they say: If we found mercy to pardon and grace to help us, if we washed away our sins in the fountain of Jesus' blood, if we were brought up from deep pit and miry clay, to sit on thrones and wear blood-bought crowns, why not you? Behold, the Lord's hand is not shortened, that it cannot save; neither his ear heavy, that it cannot hear.

III. This truth is full of comfort and encouragement—

1. To God's people.

One wonders in reading the early history of the Israelites how, after what they had seen of God's power, they could ever doubt or distrust it. We think, Had I stood beside Moses on the banks of the Nile, and seen her waters at a wave of his rod change to blood; or, girded for the journey, and listening, had I heard the cry which rose over the first-born at the midnight hour; or had I seen the gates of the sea thrown back and held open, till, walking its floor between two walls of water, I reached the other strand; or had I pitched my tent where the skies dropped not dews, nor rain, nor hoar-frost, but food on the wilderness, and made barren sands more fertile than fields of corn;—recollecting how the waters had been turned into rock, would not I have waited to see the rock turned into water, nor joined the unbelieving crew in their cries to Moses, "Give us water that we may drink. Wherefore is this that thou hast brought us up out of Egypt, to kill us and our children and our cattle with thirst?" So we judge. But may we not think more highly of ourselves than we ought to think? for as the bravest troops have sometimes been seized with a panic, or as where an epidemic rages, killing thousands, the stout and healthy who survive may yet suffer some touch of the prevailing malady, even Moses himself on one occasion gave way to despondency,—in reply to God's promise, I will give them flesh, asking, The people, among whom I am, are six hundred thousand footmen; shall the flocks and the herds be slain for them, to suffice them? or shall all the fish of the sea be gathered together for them, to suffice them?

Is the Lord's hand waxed short? was God's answer to Moses: and it is mine to all the believer's doubts, and difficulties, and fears. Since you were called, converted, first visited with saving grace, is the Lord's hand waxed short? No; then let that thought inspire you, as it did David, with dauntless faith. As with a touch of gentle pity Saul looked on the stripling who offered to do battle with the Philistine, he said, Thou art not able to go against this Philistine to fight with him: for thou art but a youth, and he a man of war from his youth. "Thy servant," was the bold reply, "kept his father's sheep, and there came a lion, and a bear, and took a lamb out of the flock: and I went out after him, and smote him, and delivered it out of his mouth: and when he arose against me, I caught him by his beard, and smote him, and slew him. Thy servant slew both the lion and the bear: and this uncircumcised Philistine shall be as one of them, seeing he hath defied the armies of the living God. The Lord that hath delivered me out of the paw of the lion, and out of the paw of the bear, he will deliver me out of the hand of this Philistine." Sound logic, as well as sound theology! And if God has graciously delivered you from the curse, shall he not deliver you from the power of sin? if he has justified, shall he not also sanctify you? if he has brought you out of Egypt, shall he not guide your steps to Canaan? He did not pluck you from the burning to throw you again into the fire. Cast your burden on the Lord, and he will sustain you. Pray, and wait the answer. As Moses said to Israel, with Egypt's hosts pressing on their rear, and the Red Sea roaring on their front: Stand still and see the salvation of the Lord. His hand is not shortened, that it cannot save; neither his ear heavy, that it cannot hear.

2. This truth is full of hope and encouragement to sinners.

In the annual Reports of hospitals we read of a certain number sent away cured, a certain number remaining under cure, and, to say nothing of the dead, of a number who have been dismissed as incurable—their cases baffling the skill of man and the power of medicine. The Great Physician knows no such class; the gospel brings glad tidings to the chief of sinners. This is a faithful saying, and worthy of all acceptation, says St Paul, that Christ Jesus came into the world to save sinners; of whom I am chief. He is able also to save them to the uttermost that come unto God by him.

People sometimes say of the dying, they were too late in calling the doctor. With the cold sweat standing like beads on the brow, the features pinched, the countenance changed, the eye glazed, the death-rattle sounding in the throat, and the last struggle begun, the skill of man is hopeless. He cures disease, not death. Alas! 'tis true; too late, too late! It is never so for Christ. David had one in his flock that he had plucked out of the lion's very jaws; but Christ has many such—many saved who were as near destruction. Tell me not, then, that you have sinned too much or too long to be saved. Is his hand shortened since the day he saved the dying thief, and set his soul free to go up to heaven, like a bird out of the fowler's snare? Look what he has done for others, and learn what he can and will do for you. Too great sinners to be saved? Hast thou with Peter looked Jesus in the face, and, cursing, said, "I know him not?" Hast thou with Saul imbrued thy hands in holy martyrs' blood? Hast thou with the thief joined thy fellows in reviling a dying Lord? Hast thou stood on Calvary to shake the head and point the finger and cry, in cruel mockery of him whom the nails fastened, and his own blood glued to the tree, If thou be the Son of God, come down! No? Then why should the door be shut against you that opened to these? Who gets to heaven will find seated on its thrones, in Abel, Enoch, Abraham, Moses, greater saints than he has been, and in others, perhaps, greater sinners. God has done more marvellous works of power and mercy than saving you. Though he had not, though you were the vilest sinner that ever polluted his beautiful earth with your feet, or profaned his holy sanctuary with your presence, you have only now, and as you are, to throw yourself at the feet of Jesus, crying, Save me, I perish—and you are saved. Then in the words of the poet—

> "Out of your last home dark and cold,
> Thou shalt pass to a city whose streets are gold;
> From the silence that falls upon sin and pain,
> To the deathless joys of the angels' strain;
> Well shall be ended what ill began,
> Out of the shadow into the sun."

IV.

THE GRACE OF FAITH.

"Now abideth faith."—1 Cor. xiii. 13.

HAST thou faith? To this, an apostle's question, all men could, in a sense, return an answer in the affirmative; for it is not more true that no man liveth and sinneth not, than that no man liveth and believeth not; or devil either, for "the devils also believe and tremble." Suppose a man without faith in any one, without faith in the honesty of his servants, faith in the integrity of his friends, faith in the affections of his children, faith in the fidelity of his wife, death would be to be preferred to a life like his. Better that our eyes were closed in death than that they should see every one with a mask on their face and a dagger beneath their cloak; with such a jaundiced vision, we should be "of all men the most miserable." On looking into the matter, you will find that faith, instead of belonging only to the elect of God, holy and chosen, is common to all, even the worst of men. The backbone, indeed, of the social, and the foundation of the commercial fabric, remove faith between man and man, and society and commerce fall to pieces. There is not a happy home on earth but stands on faith; our heads are pillowed on it; we sleep at night in its arms with greater security for the safety of our lives, peace, and property, than bolts and bars can give.

I. In illustration of the universality of faith, observe—

1. Faith, which is the source of so much human happiness, is the mainspring of human activity. It moves more than half the machinery of life. What leads the husbandman, for example, to yoke his horses when, no bud bursting to clothe the naked trees, no bird singing in hedgerows or frosty skies, nature seems dead? With faith in the regularity of her laws, in the ordinance of her God, he believes that she is not dead but sleepeth; and so he ploughs and sows in the certain expectation that he shall reap, and that these bare fields shall be green in summer with waving corn, and be merry in autumn with sun-browned reapers. The farmer is a man of faith. So is the seaman. No braver man than he who goes down to see God's wonders in the deep. Venturing his frail bark on a sea ploughed by many keels, but wearing on its bosom the furrows of none, with neither path to follow nor star to guide, the master knows no fear. When the last blue hill has dipped beneath the wave, and he is alone on a shoreless sea, he is calm and confident—his faith in the compass-needle,

which, however his ship may turn, or roll, or plunge, ever points true to the north. An example his to be followed by the Christian with his Bible, on that faith venturing his all, life, crew, and cargo, he steers his way boldly through darkest nights and stormiest oceans, with nothing but a thin plank between him and the grave. And though metaphysicians and divines have involved this matter of faith in mystery, be assured that there is nothing more needed for your salvation or mine than that God would inspire us with a belief in the declarations of his word as real, heartfelt, and practical, as that which we put in the laws of providence—in the due return of day and night, summer and winter, seed-time and harvest.

2. The followers of the world have faith. For their salvation it only needs to be rightly and divinely directed. Where will you find it stronger than in those who, in spite not only of others' sad experience, but also of their own, seek true, lasting happiness in earthly pleasures. One gourd has perished after another; the ground beneath their feet is strewed ankle deep with their withered leaves; yet see how they train up another gourd in hope of better fortune. These men might have learned, one would think, that the happiness which they expect from the possession of any earthly object is a delusion. The phantom has ever eluded their grasp; yet, as it dances on before them, they persevere; nor cease the vain pursuit, till they stumble into the grave. There is a

faith in the world which no succession of disappointments seems able to destroy, or even to disturb. It is very sad to see it! We have not to go to a heathen hell to see the Tantalus, who, though he has always found that so soon as the cup touches his thirsty lips, the water vanishes, yet ever raises it anew; or the Sisyphus, who, though the stone with sore labour has no sooner been rolled to the brow of the mountain than it has always slipped from his hands and bounded back to the bottom, yet begins again, and again, and again, the wretched task. This world is the hell where such tasks are done, such disappointments are borne; and borne often with a patience and an endurance of faith in the worldling which almost tempts us to adopt the language of our Lord, and say, We have not found so great faith, no, not in Israel! If surpassed at all, their faith in the world is only exceeded by that which Job expressed in God, when, from the ashes where he sat over the graves of his children, the patriarch lifted his eyes to heaven, to cry, Though he slay me, yet will I trust in him!

3. Unbelievers have faith, notwithstanding that that appears a contradiction in terms.

They present a still more remarkable and melancholy illustration than the last, of the fact that faith, though in one and the most important sense a special gift of God, is natural to the human heart. Many people, for instance, who do not believe in the divinity of the Bible, will be found giving credit to the ravings and wretched nonsense of *spiritualism*, as it is called. The credulity of sceptics is quite remarkable; but this is still more remarkable, that thousands who are not sceptics, though they withhold their faith from the truths of God's word, put it in these old threadbare lies of the devil—"Thou shalt not surely die;" you can sin to-day and repent to-morrow; you may turn religious at a more convenient season; it will be time enough to seek another world when this has lost its enjoyments, and "the years draw nigh when thou shalt say, I have no pleasure in them;" the evening of life, like the last quiet hours of day, is best adapted for prayer and meditation; farewell to all enjoyments so soon as you allow your attention to be occupied with such gloomy subjects as death, the grave, judgment, and eternity; banish your idle fears; God, unlike man dressed in a little brief authority, is much too generous to be an exacting judge, and too merciful to be a severe one; at any rate, should the worst come to the worst, you can reasonably calculate on a season for repentance; and you will find it much easier to attend to these things when your head is gray, and your passions are cooled, and the night's falling shadows dispose you to solemn thoughts, than it is now. By such lies as these, the cunning fiend leads thousands on, step by step, to everlasting ruin. And thus, strange as it may sound, it is true that it is as much by faith—of a kind—that some go to hell, as it is by faith that God's people go to heaven.

Therefore, as a man approaching a precipice does not need to get feet, but to get the feet he has turned round, so that every step becomes one from danger to safety, it is not so much faith we need, as that the faith we have be set on new and right objects, and turned in a new and right direction. What we need in order to be saved is the faith that, looking to Jesus, becomes saving faith—and saving because it embraces the Saviour; which has God for its author, Christ for its object, these other graces for its fruits, and for its reward a kingdom and a crown in heaven. This is the faith of which Paul says, Now abideth faith, hope, charity.

II. Let us attend to the importance of sound scriptural views of this matter.

This was never more necessary than now. Liberty of thought, of private judgment, on which our Protestantism stands, is in danger; and in danger from the conduct of rash and unwise men. Such a calamity threatens it as befell the cause of civil liberty, when the revolutionists of France, confounding licence with liberty, destroyed everything and built up nothing; and, leaving their country without a government, and by their worship of the goddess of Reason, I may add, without a God, made the very name of liberty to stink in the nostrils of the world. We are invited now-a-days, to lift those anchors of the faith by which our fathers rode out many a storm; yet it were well and wise, before doing so, to see into what position we are likely to drive. So far as concerns either the religious or civil condition of those communities from which these novelties in faith and practice have been imported, I see no reason to envy them; to copy them; or to turn a deaf ear to the prophet's warning, Stand ye in the ways, and see, and ask for the old paths, where is the good way, and walk therein, and ye shall find rest for your souls.

Men seek to soothe our very natural alarm by drawing a distinction between doctrines and duties, saying that if our life and practice are good, it is a small matter what we believe. True, and so if the stream is pure, it is a small matter that the fountain is polluted; if the fruit is good, that the tree is bad; if the vessel is rightly steered, that both compass and chart are wrong. But who ever heard of such things? Who has gathered grapes of thorns, or figs of thistles? How can a man's conduct be right if his creed be wrong—wrong, not in its accidents, but in its essence and substance? The Spartans thought theft no crime if secretly committed; and so, that being their belief, they stole. David Hume thought the same of adultery; and so, that being his belief, what hindered him, or now hinders his followers, from such a crime? The Hindu widow thinks it meritorious to give herself to the flames which consume the body of her husband;

and so, that being her belief, she mounts the pile and commits suicide. Simon Magus thought that the Holy Ghost might be bought and sold; and so, that being his belief, by the proffer of money he offered such an insult to God, that Peter indignantly exclaimed, Thy money perish with thee! Saul of Tarsus thought it was for God's glory that he should persecute the Christians; and so, that being his belief, he steeled a naturally tender heart to the claims of pity, and imbrued his hands in the blood of martyrs. It is no answer to this to tell us of men, of whom, alas! there are too many, who set much value on an orthodox creed, and little on a holy, or even moral life; who talk much of faith, but are not careful to maintain good works. What does their case prove against the importance of sound views on such high subjects as faith, salvation by grace, and redemption through the blood of Christ? It only shews that men may sin against light and conscience—no new thing, nor peculiar to Christian ages; since an old heathen has said, "I see the better, and approve; yet follow the worse."

Such importance did Martin Luther, no mean authority, attach to the doctrine of justification by faith in the blood of Christ, that he called it the article of a standing or falling Church. I subscribe to the sentiment: ceremonies, forms, and even some doctrines, are but the ornaments of the building or parts of its superstructure; but this, lying at the foundation, touches the security of all. Embodied in her creed and faithfully preached from her pulpits, this doctrine should protect any Church when assailed by the rude hand of violence. It consecrates, if I may say so, not its errors, but its life. Were we armed with power to remove such a Church, and bent on supplying its place with what might appear to be a better system, it says, as David said to Abishai, on turning aside his spear from Saul, "Destroy him not: for who can stretch forth his hand against the Lord's anointed, and be guiltless?" Whether the candidate for baptism should be immersed or sprinkled; whether that ordinance should be administered to infants or only to adults; whether, in commemorating the death of Jesus, we should sit or kneel; whether the Church should be ruled by deacons, presbyters, or bishops; whether it should be maintained at the expense of the State, or depend only on voluntary liberality; are questions on which no man will spend dying thoughts or waste dying hours. No. The nearer we approach to another world the less these questions will appear, but the greater this—Am I, being justified by faith, at peace with God through my Lord Jesus Christ? Other foundation than this can no man lay. Destroy it not! Destroy it; remove it, or rather me from my confidence in it, in Jesus Christ and him crucified as the only refuge of a sinner, and gone is my peace, my hopes in death, and my heaven in eternity,—I have suffered greater loss, I am a poorer man than he who pursued the plunderers of his shrine, crying, Ye have taken away my gods, and what have I more?

III. Salvation through faith, and not through works, is a feature peculiar to the gospel.

An atheist is a moral monster. Man has fallen, but not so low as to be satisfied with the atheist's cold, and dark, and dreary creed. Recoiling from that, he has erred on the side of a multiplicity of gods. The soul craves for a god as the body craves for food. It clings to the thought as a creeper to the pole it climbs; and, rather than his spirit should want such a support, man will catch at the wildest and most childish notion of beings above himself—just as ivy, when it has not a rock, will embrace a rotten tree, or as a drowning wretch, for lack of something better, clutches at a straw. So in the darkness amid which men were left to grope, may be found I know not how many false systems of religion. Some worship the serpent, others the crocodile; here the ox is adored, there the elephant. These Parsees, prostrating themselves before the rising sun, worship fire; while those Hindoos, believing its waters to possess a virtue capable of washing away sin, account the Ganges sacred, and regard it as divine. In yonder desert which he treads with naked foot the savage starts back, with a look and a cry of horror; he has trodden, not on a deadly serpent, but on a poor insect, which, wounded, dying, and all unconscious of the honours paid to it, he kneels to worship. Nor do the modes of heathen worship differ less than its objects. The blood of calves reeks on this altar; the blood of man on that. At the shrine of one divinity they present the golden fruits of earth, and at another the gory spoils of battle. Here, her abode beneath sunny skies, a benevolent deity is worshipped by boys and girls crowned with garlands of beautiful flowers, and dancing to the sounds of music. Another dwells in the recesses of the gloomy forest; his temple a circle of rude and roofless stones, and the offering for his worship a young and lovely maiden, who fills the woods with unavailing shrieks as cruel priests drag her to the altar which she is to dye with blood.

Yet, different as these religions are, they have one feature in common. In every case the worshipper expected, by his works, offerings, or sufferings, to be his own Saviour. Ask yon Hindoo, for instance, who has lain for long years on a bed of iron spikes, or held up his arm till it has become rigid and withered like the blasted branch of a living tree, or travels painfully on his knees to the distant shrine of a favourite god, why this pain, these horrid, self-inflicted tortures? They have one answer. Through these, reproaching our indolence, and apathy, and self-indulgence, and ready with the men of Tyre and Sidon to rise up to condemn many of us in the day of judgment, they expect to purchase pardon and to open the gates of Paradise. Since men never yet corrupted, as you see in Popery, the true religion, nor, as you see in Paganism, invented a false one, but the great, prominent doctrine of their creed was salvation through works, the gospel in proclaiming salvation, not through merit, or by works, but by faith, stands out in a character all its own. It is thus as much distinguished from common creeds as was its author, a virgin's child, from common men; and we may apply to his gospel the very words spoken of himself—whether he spoke peace to a troubled bosom or to a stormy sea, bade the water turn into wine, or the dead corpse into life, it could be said of Jesus, Never man spake like this man. What other religion ever spake such words, offered salvation to the lost on such terms as these—sent forth a cry like that which is echoing from pole to pole and ringing round the world, Ho, every one that thirsteth, come ye to the waters, and he that hath no money; come ye, buy, and eat; yea, come, buy wine and milk without money and without price: Believe on the Lord Jesus Christ, and thou shalt be saved: Come unto me, all ye that labour and are heavy laden, and I will give you rest: Not by works of righteousness which we have done, but according to his mercy he saved us, by the washing of regeneration and renewing of the Holy Ghost. Blessed sayings! faithful as blessed, they are worthy of all acceptation!

IV. Salvation through faith dislodges and sweeps away all confidence in our own works. The gospel, as I could most clearly shew, while resting all on faith, recognises the importance of good works; insists on the performance of them; and regards them, indeed, as the only trustworthy evidence of conversion—"the tree is known by his fruit." Still it does not recognise, but sweeps them away as grounds of a sinner's justification in the sight of God and acquittal at the bar of judgment. I know no more remarkable illustration of this than is found in the history of that eminent Reformer to whom I have already referred. One day, while he was reading the Bible, Luther's eye caught these words—The just shall live by faith; and out of that sentence, as from a little seed, the Reformation sprang. It fell into his mind as an acorn drops into the soil beneath which it bursts its shell, and rising a tender shoot, grows up into an oak that flourishes in the sunshine of a thousand summers, and defies the storms of a thousand winters. By God's blessing on these few words, Luther broke loose from the trammels of Popery, a freeman whom the truth makes free. With these, as with a wedge, Heaven lending him strength and courage to drive it home, he split up and shivered into fragments the strong and hoary system of Romish superstition. "The just shall live by faith!" Shall he? Then if eternal life is by faith and not by works, man is not saved by penance—and he swept that away; nor by the merits of saints—and he swept those away; nor by indulgences, nor by fasts and vigils, the voluntary poverty and the sackcloth, the pilgrimages and the prayers of the Church of Rome—and he swept all away. Thus working, as they say, with a will, with stout heart and strong arm, Martin Luther cleared away the rubbish which had been gathering for long ages above the true foundation of a sinner's acceptance with a righteous God; and on, and deeper on, he wrought, till he reached and laid bare the rock. That Rock was Christ; and there a jubilant world read these words, written by the finger of God, in letters large and legible—Other foundation can no man lay than that is laid, which is Jesus Christ.

V. The practical conclusion is, that while we are to abound in the work of the Lord, and be careful to maintain good works, we are to be no less careful not to trust in them. The two are quite compatible—incompatible as they seemed to one who, speaking of a distinguished saint, said, I do not understand him; he speaks of his good works as filthy rags, yet no man takes such care to cover himself with such rags. How compatible they are, appeared also in that chamber where, while the last hours of faith and piety were offering the grandest spectacle beneath the sun, a bystander reminded the dying Christian of the good that he had done, of his holy, useful, and illustrious life. He bade him cease—saying, I take my good works and my bad works, and, casting them into one heap, turn from both to Christ. Faith in an unseen Saviour is, I admit, not easy. It is our nature to walk by sight rather than by faith; and the gift of God, faith, is acquired "not by might, nor by power, but by my Spirit, saith the Lord of hosts."

A boy once threw himself down from the upper window of a house on fire into his father's arms. He did not see him; from the ledge where, hesitating to leap, he stood till it burned beneath his feet, he saw only the smoke rolling between them, pierced with tongues of flame. But up through that suffocating, sulphurous cloud, high above the roar of the rising flames, he heard and recognised his father's voice—crying, in urgent, imploring tone, Leap for your life! I am below to receive you into my arms. And when, confident in his father's word, and love, and power, he sprang from the height, right into the lurid darkness, it was a brave leap—a grand act of faith. Still, he had the evidence of sound, he heard his father's voice. And yon old man had the evidence of sight, when, taking the babe from Mary's arms into his own, he bowed his head, and raising it to heaven, exclaimed, Lord, now lettest thou thy servant depart in peace, according to thy word: for mine eyes have seen thy salvation. Simeon saw the tree in the tender shoot; the day in the opening dawn; in the little cloud no bigger than a man's hand the whole heavens overspread by thickest vapours, and pouring down such rain on the thirsty ground that streams burst foaming from the hills, and deserts were pools of water. Not so our eyes and ears! We never saw our Saviour's face: we never heard our Father's voice.

Faith here achieves what in other things would be impossibilities, and what in earthly affairs would be regarded as the height of rashness. In Jesus Christ, whom having not seen we love, we believe in one we never saw; and in our souls we commit the keeping of our most precious treasure to one who dwells in a remote and unknown land—a country from which no traveller has ever returned to assure us that his trust was not, and that ours will not, be misplaced.

Yet blessed are they that have not seen and yet have believed. The seen are shadows; the substance is found in the unseen. These are the most real objects—God, whom no man ever saw and lived; the soul, which does not grow infirm with time and defies the sharpest darts of death; not this world of matter, which shall vanish in the smoke of its own funereal fires, but that world of spirits, where saints enjoy a glory that never fades and crowns that never fall, and sinners suffer the worm that never dies and the fire that is never quenched. No doubt, in Christ the foundation of our faith is unseen; but so is that of yonder tower that lifts its tall erect form among the waves over which it throws a saving light. It appears to rest on the rolling billows; but beneath these, invisible and immovable, lies the solid rock on which it stands secure; and when the hurricane roars above, and breakers roar below, and ships are wrecking, and men are drowning, and women are weeping, I could go calmly to sleep in that lone sea-tower. Founded on a rock, and safer than the proudest palace that stands on the sandy, surf-beaten shore, it cannot be moved. Still less the Rock of Ages! Who trusts in that is fit for death, prepared for judgment, ready for the last day's sounding trumpet, since the Lord redeemeth the soul of his servants; and none of them that trust in him shall be desolate. Happy is that people that is in such a case: yea, happy is that people whose God is the Lord.

V.

THE GRACE OF FAITH.

"Now abideth faith."—1 Cor. xiii. 13.

ON a Sabbath-day, years ago, a young minister appeared in a church of this city as a candidate for the vacant charge. He preached; the people were all attention. The discourse was worthy of one whose ministrations since then have been elsewhere much blessed to bring many souls to Christ. That did not save it, however, from the adverse judgment of a critic. So soon as the sermon was concluded, this modern Athenian turned round to him who related the circumstance, and said, with a shrug of his shoulders, and a tone bordering on contempt, Ha! there is nothing new there! Fancy a man to whom I offer a rose fresh plucked from the parterre, dyed in the richest hues, breathing the most fragrant odour, with the dew-drops still shining like diamonds on its pure bosom, tossing it from him with an air of contempt, to say, Ah! there is nothing new there! This were not more absurd than that. New? Anything in religion that professes to be new, beyond the light which modern researches into the geography and natural history, the manners, customs, and languages of the East, may throw on the contents of the Bible, is to be regarded with grave suspicion; and, since the tendency of our times is to leave the old paths, and seek for something new—

I. Let me exhort those in whom faith abideth, to abide in the faith.

It is not much more than a century since Galvani, a native of Bologna, happened one day to bring two metals in contact with the limb of a dead frog. It quivered. The result was the discovery of a power whereby, making us able to annihilate space, rival the flight of time, and so flash our thoughts through the bosom of the ocean and the bowels of the earth, we can send a message and get an answer almost as soon from the capital of Russia as from the house of an acquaintance in the street next to our own. Modern facts are more wonderful than old fables. It is not even one century since Benjamin Franklin, by means of a child's plaything, entered, if I may say so, the bosom of the cloud, and, seizing the thunderbolt, returned with it to the earth, like a magician who has thrown his spell on some mighty spirit, and bound it to his service. Every day almost presents us with some new invention, and science is ever and anon interesting its votaries by some new discovery, or startling the world by some strange one. We know what our forefathers never so much as dreamed of,—

that there are metals which swim on the top of water, and take fire at the touch of snow—that the diamond which flashes on a lady's finger is but a bit of coal—that the pearls which gem a royal crown are but the excrescences of disease—that the water which we employ to extinguish fire is composed of two elements which burn with the brightest light and fiercest heat—and that there is thus stored up in the sea itself a magazine of combustibles sufficient, when God shall kindle them, to wrap this world in flames, and turn it to a heap of ashes. In new planets and comets, new plants and animals, new metals and earths, science is adding page on page to the volume of nature's wonders, teaching the Christian to kneel before the Lord our Maker, and exclaim with deeper, devouter feelings, The earth is full of thy glory—the earth is full of thy riches. Such progress has the world made since the days of Solomon, that, were he to return to the scene of his former studies, he would no longer be a wonder queens might go to see, but, in point of knowledge, would stand below some whom we count little better than fools. Indeed, there is not a boy whom you meet in a morning, creeping with satchel on his back to school, but knows much that even Newton did not know, and is familiar with facts which would have excited the astonishment, perhaps the doubts, of that prince of philosophers.

How different the region of religion! and different because our faith has been revealed from heaven. Inspired of God, it is intended not for the learned and wise only, but also for the humble and the poor; complete—nothing can be added to it; perfect—nothing can be taken from it; plain—there is line upon line, precept upon precept, here a little and there a little; intelligible to the humblest understanding, he who runs may read, and the wayfaring man, though a fool, shall not err therein. Since the days when heads now gray were black, since mothers were girls and men were boys, discoveries have been made in science which would have astonished Newton; but during the last eighteen centuries has anything been discovered in the Bible that would have astonished Paul? Since the beloved disciple closed this volume on the shores of Patmos, has one line been added to the Word of God, one doctrine or one duty been discovered there with which he was not acquainted? I know nothing in the writings of modern theologians that would have astonished the apostles but the audacity with which, not avowed infidels, but professed Christians, have treated their characters and their writings. We are to search the Scriptures with the eagerness of one who digs for hidden treasure. But this field is not like those gold regions on Californian coasts or the Australian continent which, left for long ages to the lowest savages, have been but recently explored. The road to heaven has been too long travelled by the feet of devout men, and too carefully surveyed and examined by them on their knees, for anything of importance to have escaped their notice. Long as familiar to the wise and good, as the path between a cottage door and cottage well, there is nothing in the world so improbable as that the gospel of Jesus Christ will yield anything new in matters either of doctrine or duty to the keenest or most curious eye; and therefore, though inapplicable to works on science or art, to books of theology, to systems of doctrine, or codes of duty that pretend to set forth discoveries in the Word of God, we may safely apply the adage, What is new in them is not true, and what is true is not new.*

It is not the practice of Protestants blindly to follow any leader, to pin their faith to church or churchmen. Like the Bereans of old, who were therefore more honourable than those of Thessalonica, we regard it as a duty, and claim it also as a right, to bring everything to the test of God's Word; and with all due respect to the creeds of Churches and the writings of the Fathers, to search the Scriptures whether these things

---

* "I believe," said Webster, the great American statesman, "that the Bible is to be understood and received in the plain and obvious meaning of its passages; since I cannot persuade myself that a book intended for the instruction and conversion of the whole world should cover its true meaning in such mystery and doubt that none but critics and philosophers can discover it; and believe that the experiments and subtleties of human wisdom are more likely to obscure than to enlighten the revealed will of God, and that he is the most accomplished Christian scholar who hath been educated at the feet of Jesus, and in the College of Fishermen."

are so. Still, he is a fool who, travelling over desert, moor, or mountain, allows himself to be easily persuaded to leave the beaten track for some new untrodden way. Depend on it that the old path which men with the Word of God in their hands and his grace in their hearts, took to serve him in this world, and to dwell with him in heaven in the next, is the right one. By abiding in their old path, we are most likely to abide in the true faith. Such is the very counsel which Christ himself gives to the Church, when, in the Song of Songs, she asks, Tell me, O thou whom my soul loveth, where thou feedest, where thou makest thy flock to rest at noon? If thou know not, he replies, O thou fairest among women, go thy way forth by the footsteps of the flock. God expresses himself to the very same effect by the prophet in a figure drawn from pastoral life, and intelligible to all who are in any measure familiar with the scenery of our glens and the habits of the sheep. Wherever they have to skirt a precipice, or wind through the black morass, they march in single file, and stick to the old, beaten path, trodden down and marked even on scattered stones and outlying rock by the feet of generations that have gone before; and referring to this, God addresses his people thus—"Stand ye in the ways, and see, and ask for the old paths, where is the good way, and walk therein, and ye shall find rest for your souls." And so shall we, in the old ways of keeping the Sabbath, amid the quiet observances of that hallowed day; and so shall we likewise, in the old faith of "Jesus Christ and him crucified," safely and sweetly sheltered from every storm in the clefts of that Rock of Ages.

II. Salvation through faith in the righteousness of Jesus Christ does not supersede the use of means.

A heathen relates how he, when about to set sail on a dangerous voyage, selected the best ship, manned her with the stoutest crew, chose the most propitious season of the year for the enterprise; and that after having done this, all that man could do, he committed himself to the protection of the gods. Were it needful to learn from a heathen, this old worshipper of the false might teach us how to trust in the true God—both for the bounties of providence and the blessings of grace. Faith is undoubtedly the gift of God, the work of the Spirit, and the answer to prayer. But, if the necessity of looking above ourselves for ability to believe, be clear, and if it be plain from the Word of God, that we cannot depend too much on Divine strength, it is equally evident that we cannot be too diligent in using the means of Divine appointment. "I can do all things," says Paul, "through Christ which strengtheneth me,"—this his bold yet modest confidence, not that Christ would do the things, but would strengthen him to do them.

Therefore we ought to work at least as diligently for spiritual as for temporal mercies. But we do not.

Alas! Who does? In proportion to their importance, who gives as much time to prayer as to business; as much thought to their Bibles as merchants to their ledgers; as much trouble to cultivate their souls as husbandmen expend in ploughing and sowing and weeding the soil, and reaping the crop? No wonder that many are lost; they take no trouble to be saved. And no wonder that even those who are saved make such slow progress in the divine life, that they find self-examination to be such an unpleasant task, and that their Christian course corresponds so little to the beautiful and familiar image of the shining light that shineth more and more unto the perfect day. Making the doctrine of man's inability an excuse for sloth and idleness, we seem to entertain the vague and vain expectation that we shall be borne onwards to heaven like a boat without sail or oar on the bosom of a flowing tide; and that, instead of having laboriously to climb the ladder, hand over hand, we shall somehow or other rise to glory as in angels' arms and on angels' wings. Is this to honour the grace of God? Certainly not. The diligent and anxious use of means casts no reflection or disparagement on the doctrine of faith, of salvation not by the law, but by grace. What madness is it for a man to rush naked into a battle-field? It is he who arms himself for the combat, and none else, that honours the Providence without whose permission not a hair of his head shall be touched, though he charge up to the cannon's mouth, or throw himself headlong into the fiery breach. It is the ship that has a steersman at her wheel, and an outlook on the bows, that sails under the flag of Providence—owning and honouring him who doth fly upon the wings of the wind and hath measured the waters in the hollow of his hand. That is faith; anything else is presumption, and can only end in a miserable shipwreck. Who, for instance, considers himself guilty of mistrusting the promise, Thy bread shall be given thee, and thy water shall be sure, by toiling at his work? There is not more harmony between the divine perfections, between the Old and New Testaments, between the songs of saints and angels, than there is between the prayer for bread on a good man's lips, and the sweat of honest labour on his brow; between the hard toil of the field and the hopeful trust of the closet. And, in calling on you, in entreating and urging you to put on the whole armour of God, to watch and pray, to guard against temptation, to flee youthful lusts, to depart from all iniquity, to give all diligence to make your calling sure, to work out your salvation with fear and trembling, I am no more casting a doubt on salvation by grace than I am denying a presiding Providence when I tell a youth about to go out into the world that "the hand of the diligent maketh rich," and that unless he work, "poverty" shall "come as one that travelleth, and want as an armed man."

The Grace of Faith.

III. Consider how faith is a saving grace.

Can faith save him? says St James, speaking of one who says he has faith, but not works. Certainly not; for I no more believe in the reality of a faith without works, than of a fire without heat. But assuming the faith to be genuine, Can faith save him? Well, it can, and it cannot. In explanation of this, I remark—

1. It is not by our faith, but by Christ's righteousness, that we are justified.

To illustrate this, let me recall two incidents in our Saviour's history. He is standing one day by the shore of Galilee, when the lake, dotted with the white sails of fishing-boats, spreads itself out at his feet, and over his head a sycamine throws its branches, yielding a grateful shade from the heat of the burning sun. To a prayer of his disciples, which we would all do well to offer—Increase our faith, he returned this remarkable reply, If ye had faith as a grain of mustard seed, ye might say unto this sycamine tree, Be thou plucked up by the root, and be thou planted in the sea; and it should obey you. Suppose that they, retreating to a safe distance, had tried the bold experiment, and with such success as Peter's, when, in the strength of faith, he leaped from the boat to stand erect on the rolling billow, and advanced, stepping from wave to wave, to meet his Master. Fancy this, and that the people, with wondering eyes, saw the sycamine, as by whirlwind power, torn up from the ground, rise like a balloon, sail through the air with leafy branches and naked roots, till, having been lowered slowly down, it buried its roots in the bosom of the waters, and stood there upright, firm, green as its neighbours on the shore. Might they not have pointed to the tree growing where never tree grew before, to say, See what faith has done! Yet faith had not done it. How could that which is but a feeling in the mind, reverse the laws of nature, and, plucking up a mighty tree, plant its roots as firmly in water as when they were anchored in the soil, or matted around a rock. Faith accomplishes the work only by bringing into play the power of God; as, to use a humble comparison, even a child can turn a gigantic wheel by opening the sluice, and letting the water on.

Or take, in illustration, a case that actually occurred. On another day our Lord is in a crowd. A woman, who has long suffered from an incurable disease, edges her way through the throng; and stooping down, unseen, reaches out her hand to touch the hem of his garment, and rises cured of the bloody issue. As she retreats, his voice arrests her. Trembling, she retraces her steps, and approaches him to hear these blessed words, Daughter, be of good comfort; thy faith hath made thee whole. Such is Matthew's account of the transaction. Mark throws further light on it, and on the point before us. According to his account, so soon as the woman touched our Lord, in an instant, suddenly as one who feels the stab of a knife, or the hand that steals his purse in a crowd, Jesus faces round on the throng, to demand, "Who touched my clothes?" The disciples were surprised; the woman was alarmed; and, knowing herself to be the culprit, if this was a crime, she came, in the words of the Evangelist, fearing and trembling, knowing what was done in her, and fell down before him, and told him all the truth. Now, what made Jesus ask a question, apparently so unreasonable that his own disciples remonstrated with him, saying, Thou seest the multitude thronging thee, and sayest thou, Who touched me? Mark tells us the why and wherefore. He states, that our Saviour knew that virtue, or, as we should now say, power, had gone out of him. This it was—not her touch, nor his garment, nor her faith, but the power that had gone out of him, that cured the woman; just as it is the water, not the cup, that quenches the thirst; the medicine, not the hand that takes it, nor the faith that swallows it, which arrests my malady, and saves my life; or, as when I place my finger on the ball of a Leyden jar, it is the subtle, invisible, electric fluid enclosed within its crystal walls, that, discharged by the touch, sends a shock thrilling through my frame. Even so, notwithstanding that it is said, Being justified by faith, we have peace with God, it is not faith, but the virtue which faith draws out of Christ, that justifies us; in other words, that righteousness which he wrought out when, taking our sins on himself, as man's substitute, he bore their punishment; and taking our obligations on himself, he performed our duty, and paid all our debt.

This righteousness is not imputed in any case because it is deserved; but imputed, thank God, in every case where it is sincerely desired. Whosoever, however unworthy he be, is willing to receive Christ as his Saviour, as well from the power as from the punishment of sin—whosoever, in other words, believeth in him shall not perish, but have everlasting life. Jesus stands in the presence of every congregation, willing and mighty to save, as on the day when he looked on the woman who lay trembling at his feet, to address her in the language of tender affection, and calm the tumult of her soul with these blessed words, Daughter, be of good comfort; thy faith hath made thee whole. Were we as prompt as she was to seize the opportunity, our humility would be crowned with still greater honours, and our faith with a more enduring reward.

2. While we are not saved by faith, it is through faith only that we receive the righteousness of Jesus Christ.

There are two arts, the one simple and very old, the other very complex, but modern, which are illustrative of important Bible truths. We have, like Jeremiah, in the words of Scripture, gone down to the potter's house, and, behold, he wrought a work on the wheels. Before him is a revolving horizontal disk; beside him a heap of clay. Seizing a handful of the clay, he throws it down, a rude, unformed, shapeless mass, on the flying wheel; and how curious it is to see that lump, as it spins round and round, begin at the touch of his skilful fingers to lose its shapelessness, assume a definite form, and by and by swell out and rise up into a vessel of perfect proportions. It is more than curious; it is instructive. One cannot watch the plastic clay growing to the workman's will and touch into a vessel of honour or dishonour, for common or sacred uses, for roughest hands or jewelled fingers, without seeing God in the potter, and man in the clay—feeling the beauty of Scripture figures, and how much ourselves and fortunes are in the hands of him who said, "O house of Israel, cannot I do with you as this potter? saith the Lord. Behold, as the clay is in the potter's hand, so are ye in mine hand, O house of Israel."—Shall the thing made say of him that made it, Why hast thou made me thus?

An art much more complex and modern than the potter's may supply us with an illustration of salvation through the transference of righteousness from the Saviour to the sinner. Before you stands a bath, as it is called, a large vessel full of acid liquor. At one end, immersed in the fluid, hangs a sheet of silver; while above, and passing from side to side, is extended a thread of metal, ready to be connected with a powerful battery, which, when I saw the process, was concealed in a room below. A vessel of common metal being produced, was hung on the wire and plunged into the bath, in which, I may remark, the fluid was so clear, that you could see to the bottom. The wire on which it was suspended was then connected with the electric battery; and what happened? A very remarkable result. By means of the mighty though unseen agent that was thus brought into action, the particles of silver were taken from the sheet of it, and, passing invisibly through the translucent fluid, were transferred to the vessel that had been immersed in the bath. No sound accompanied the mysterious process, no violent action, no sign of motion; the eye saw nothing but the dull metal beginning to assume a brilliant appearance, and in time, through what looked more like magic than common art, this base vessel shone in a coating of the purest silver. Such change, but far greater and more thorough, is wrought on the soul through the unseen and almighty influences of the Holy Spirit, so soon as faith has established a connexion between the Saviour and the sinner. Righteousness is withdrawn from the former and transferred to the latter. In the words of an inspired apostle, the believer puts on Christ—to stand before God covered with those merits, and justified by that righteousness which makes a sinner just.

If this process of art suggested that resemblance, it presented under one aspect a mighty difference. Robbed of its precious metal, what was once a sheet of silver became in time a dull, attenuated, worthless thing. Its treasures were exhausted; Christ's never are. It could coat and cover a certain number;

no more. But in him there is righteousness sufficient for all the world; and, with enough of mercy in the Father, of merit in the Son, and of grace in the Spirit, oh! why should there be one of us, one child of guilt and sin, of whom it cannot, as it might, be said, Blessed is he whose transgression is forgiven, whose sin is covered? It were easier to empty the sun of his light, or the ocean of her waters, than Jesus of merits which are as free to all as is that sun and sea. In him dwelleth all the fulness of the Godhead bodily.

May that encourage you to go to Jesus. When?—
—now. Where?—here. How?—just as you are. Pharaoh's message found Joseph in prison, and in a prison dress; nor did the black, begrimed, bearded tenant of a dungeon, venture to present himself before the impatient king till he had "shaved himself and changed his raiment." Must we likewise wait till our habits are changed ere, responding to his call, we go to Jesus? By no means. Go as you are, just as you are. There is no need for good works at this stage, nor may there be time for them—little more time for you than for the dying thief who threw himself on bleeding mercy, and, clasped in Jesus' arms, was borne on his bosom to the gates of Paradise. May God help you to adopt the sentiments of this precious hymn:—

> " Just as I am, without one plea,
> But that thy blood was shed for me,
> And that thou bidst me come to thee;
> O Lamb of God, I come!

"Just as I am, and waiting not
To rid my soul of one dark blot,
To thee, whose blood can cleanse each spot;
    O Lamb of God, I come!

"Just as I am, though toss'd about
With many a conflict, many a doubt,
Fightings and fears within, without;
    O Lamb of God, I come!

"Just as I am, poor, wretched, blind,
Sight, riches, healing of the mind,
Yea, all I need, in thee to find;
    O Lamb of God, I come!

"Just as I am, thou wilt receive,
Wilt welcome, pardon, cleanse, relieve;
Because thy promise I believe,
    O Lamb of God, I come!"

VI.

THE GRACE OF HOPE.

"Now abideth hope."—1 COR. xiii. 13.

IT is related of Lord Nelson when a child that, on his mother telling him not to expose himself to some danger, but to fear it, he turned round to her saying, Mother, what is fear?—there the boy was indeed father to the man, who, brave even to rashness, stept on the quarter-deck of the *Victory* for his last battle wearing all his orders ; a glittering mark for the bullets of the enemy. But strangers as some may be to fear, who ever asked, What is Hope? Kings and beggars, saints and sinners, childhood, youth, manhood, and old age, all have tasted her pleasures ; and the motto on the crest of one of our old families, *Dum spiro spero*, While I breathe I hope, is one that may be adopted by the whole human race. To expect when circumstances are at the worst that they will become better, ay, and better when at the best, is as natural to us as it is to breathe.

Hope presided at all our births ; and in yonder mother whose busy fancy is weaving a bright future for her child, she rocks the infant's cradle. Other pleasures, like streams which summer dries or winter freezes, fail us; hers never—like the waters of the smitten rock, they follow us to the close of life. Constant as the emblem of God's presence to the wandering host, the pillar that was a cloud by day and a fire by night, she accompanies us to the end of our pilgrimage. Hovering like an angel over the bed of death, she often stays when physicians leave; and lingering in the bosoms of beloved ones while there is breath to move a feather, only departs with the sigh with which, as if unwilling to part, the body yields up its soul into the hands of God. God be thanked for Hope!

Often, it is true, but a fair enchantress, still she has been the parent of noble deeds; of patriots' and martyrs' heroic struggles; of the Church's and the world's greatest and boldest enterprises. Lighting up the dark future, and supporting thousands of afflicted and tried ones, of poor, hard-working, heavily-burdened men and women, who were ready to sink beneath their load, to her the world owes a large, perhaps the largest, measure of its happiness. She throws her bow on the stormiest cloud, and kindles her star in the darkest sky; for the deadliest malady she has a medicine, and for the deepest wound a balm. It is under her flag the exile sails; and beneath her banner that the soldier fights. By her lamp the pale student pursues his midnight toils. In husbandmen it is she who ploughs the wintry fields, and in seamen the watery deep. Hers is the brightest beam that shines into the captive's dungeon; and hers the hand that smooths life's thorniest pillow. She brings the wanderer home; she gives back the fallen one to a mother's arms, and to the eyes of a father mourning a long-lost son, she presents a vision of the wreck, though broken and shattered, steering to its haven— the returned prodigal weeps on his father's bosom, the fatted calf smokes on the board, music wakes up that long-silent house, and floors shake to the dancers' feet. This world's good Samaritan, Hope pours her wine and oil into the wounds of humanity; and, approaching the miserable in the mercy and might of him who came to Jericho, she casts a healing virtue into misfortune's bitterest springs. This world without Hope would be a world without a sun.

The darkest hour is that before the dawn; when things are at the worst they mend; the longest road has a turning—so Hope bravely speaks to all. And some there are whom no misfortunes seem able to overwhelm; blessed with a happy, hopeful, temperament, they ride the waves of adverse fortune like a sea-buoy, which, though submerged one moment, is up the next, mounted on the back of the billow that broke over it. No doubt, a large proportion of our hopes suffer the fate of these billows, so soon as, rolling landward, they meet the shore, and breaking, are dashed into froth and foam. But thanks be to God, that never hinders us from forming new hopes as yonder sea new waves, that, rising from its bosom, succeed each other so rapidly that one is no sooner broken than another comes rolling joyously in.

Now, if the hopes that are followed by disappointment are better than gloomy despair, if skies lighted only by dying meteors are better than utter darkness, if nights of happy dreams are better than days of dull despondency, how much better, and how blessed the hope of my text. She springs from faith, and aspires to heaven. Born of the promises of a faithful God, and never doomed to disappointment, she finds in her dying grasp no fleeting shadow, but an immortal crown.

Let us consider—

I. The object of this hope—immortality; which is,
1. The hope of nature.

All nations, whether barbarous or civilised, have cherished this hope; and, even when they shrank from the grave, have regarded it as but a gloomy passage to another and an eternal world. It was left to the infidels of Paris, amidst the ungodliness of their bloody Revolution, to inscribe over the gate of their cemetery the sentiment, Death is an eternal sleep. Among the rudest pagans death never quenched the hope of immortality. That hope rose over the grave, shining to weeping eyes, like the evening star above the place where the sun had gone down. They saw the body turned into cold, unconscious clay; they saw it wither into a whitened skeleton; they saw it moulder into a heap of dust; yet, despite these changes, the power of death, and the foul ravages of the tomb, hope, tenacious of her hold, clung to immortality. This hope was not shaken by the convulsions of dissolution; it did not expire with the passing breath; it was not buried in the dead man's tomb. If buried, it sprang like the flowers that bloomed above the sod; but not to wither and die with them.

There is no nation that does not shew some evidence of such a hope. It breathes in the prayers and flowers which are offered by the Chinese to the manes of their departed ancestors. It is painted in those pictures of a final judgment that are found on Egypt's oldest tombs. It shone in the lamps that lighted the sepulchres of Greece and Rome. It triumphed over death in the evergreen wreaths which they hung on their tombs. And nowhere is this blessed hope more distinctly expressed than at yon forest grave, where plumed and painted and silent warriors bury with his body the bow and arrows of the Indian, that his spirit might follow the chase in the land of spirits. The conclusion I draw from these things is, that hopes of immortality are as natural to the human heart as are those seeds to the soil which spring up so soon as it is stirred, and quickened into activity by the influences of light and air. Like these, they were planted by no human hand; they are the gift of God.

This belief, that in its universality presents the character of an instinct or intuition, found in remarkable analogies what nursed its hopes, and were their props, though not their parents. Men saw an image of death in sleep—the closed eyes, the dull ears, the speechless lips, the unimpassioned countenance, the prone form, the profound unconsciousness of all life's griefs, or joys, or cares; and to some happy genius, might not sleep's awakening suggest another?—the thought that as sleep is a short death, so death may be a long sleep. Might not this truth burst on a thoughtful savage at the moment of sunrise? Standing on the shore, yesterday at even, he saw the declining sun sink, full-orbed, in the western waves, and expire amid a flood of glory, unshorn of a beam; and to-day, after a period of darkness, he hails his rise, as, with ever-fresh light and splendour, he climbs the eastern heavens, to bathe hill and dale, shore and waves, with gold. And why, might he not ask, may it not be so with the spirit that, retaining its faculties to the last, and strong amid the body's decay, sank, full-orbed also, into the darkness and night of death? May it not have gone, like that sun, to shine in other lands—perhaps, after long years of absence, to return and shine once more in this?

The wish might have been father to the thought; but might not the yearly revival of nature have suggested to some the hope of a resurrection, though, when proclaimed by Paul, that doctrine startled all, and shocked some of, the men of Athens? Winter surrounded them with the emblems of death; trees turned into naked skeletons; the sweet flowers all gone; unbroken silence in groves and skies; every stream glazed like a dead man's eye, and motionless in the frost's embrace; and the earth lying stiff and cold beneath its shroud of snow. And when spring returns to clothe the trees anew, and the flowers spring up to bloom upon their graves, and songs, breaking the long silence, burst forth afresh from skies and woodlands, might not a mother, hanging over her dead, fancy that her flower also would bloom again, and some future day restore the lost one, breaking the seal of death and silence of the tomb? These things they might see through a glass darkly.

2. The object of hope is immortality as clearly revealed in the Word of God.

What was once probable, is now certain. The heathens had immortality in its shadow; we have the substance. It is not a fancy now, but a certainty. Life and immortality, the objects of a believer's hope, are clearly brought to light by the gospel; and that grand old prophecy is fulfilled, was fulfilled on the cross by its expiring, yet rejoicing and conquering victim, "O death, I will be thy plagues; O grave, I will be thy destruction." The object of this hope, the grandest man can cherish, or mind aspire to, allies us to him 'who is the same yesterday, to-day, for ever; whose life knows no end and his happiness no change. It is not that life which, brief as it is, men dread to lose, and the dying would buy at the price of a fortune; which the woman in the gospel spent all she had to preserve; which kings account of greater value than their crowns; nobles, than their titles; a miser, than his glittering heaps of gold. The hope of the Christian is immortal life—the purchase of a Saviour's blood,—the boon which God that cannot lie promised before the world began. It is begun on earth, for in the germs and seeds of it, he that believeth, as the Bible says, hath eternal life—much as the tree has the leaves and flowers of next year wrapped up in the buds of this. Commenced at the new birth, and consummated in the hour of death, it is enjoyed in that world where there is neither woe, nor want; nor griefs, nor graves; nor sickness of body, nor sorrow of heart; nor cares, nor sighs, nor sin; where the crown hides no thorn, and the heart bleeds from no secret wound; the sky wears no cloud, and day never darkens into night. Into such blessedness believers enter at death. Such blessedness has their God and Saviour laid up for all those that love him. Instead of being reluctant, the wonder is that we are not impatient to depart, saying, as we raise our eyes to those realms of bliss from this chequered and sinful world, Oh that I had wings like a dove! for then would I fly away, and be at rest.

II. Consider the source of this hope.

On opening an Etruscan tomb they found it occu-

The Grace of Hope. 99

pied by the skeleton of a king. After thousands of years of sepulture, he still wore, amid the gloom of the grave, a memorial of his former state. The skull was bound round with a fillet of gold, a remnant of his past greatness, and a bitter mockery of his present condition. Such a crown man wears in his hopes of eternal life; these, like the indestructible gold of the royal tomb, have survived his fall, and are little else now than the vestiges of departed glory. Then, bereft of power to be or to do good, of the purity of his nature, and his peace with God, man lost all true life, and became " dead in trespasses and sins." Those hopes of happiness beyond the grave, in which, whether Pagan, or careless, unconverted Christian, he now indulges, delights, wraps himself up, are but the ivy that, clothing, conceals a ruin; or, by folding a green mantle around its trunk, gives the appearance of life to a dead and withered tree.

I believe that no man lives in utter, blank, black despair. Voyaging to hell or heaven, to the haven of rest or to a fearful wrecking, every one carries hope in his heart, as all our ships do her symbol—the anchor hung at their bows. Who believe that they shall be lost when they die? None. Who lives a life of sin in this world without some expectation of escaping its punishment in the next? None; not the lowest, basest, vilest slave of vice. If men believed that death was the end of their existence, that there was no hereafter, they might toss the reins on the neck of passion

—this their motto, "A short life and a merry one!" or, as they raised the foaming cup, this, "Let us eat and drink; for to-morrow we shall die." But no man says, or could say, Let us eat and drink, for to-morrow we shall be in hell. It is no more in human nature to quaff the cup and toy with pleasure under such dread feelings, than it was in Damocles to linger at the banquet when he discovered a sword above his head, hung from the roof by a single hair. The worst have hope. Tenacious of life, she can live in an atmosphere that is fatal to every human virtue. She blooms on the grave, where all innocence, and beauty, and grace lie buried; a phenomenon more wonderful to behold than the rose of the Alps, with its roots planted on the edge of the glacier, and its arms, thickly covered with blushing flowers, thrown on a wreath of snow.

And what is the source, what are the foundations of hopes by which many are deceived till, like the rich man, they lift up their eyes in torment? Here they are; judge ye what they are worth, and see that they are not yours—God, they say, is merciful; we have been guilty, no doubt, of many bad actions, but we have done some good ones; if we are not what we should be, we are not so bad as we might have been, or as some others are; if God did not mean us to indulge our appetites, why did he give them? he does not, cannot expect perfection from those in whom he has planted passions more powerful than reason, and whom he has placed in circumstances of all but irresistible

The Grace of Hope.

temptation; youth must sow its wild oats; we will grow better as we grow older, and find leisure to repent before we die! Thus, fed by the devil's hand, that of others, or their own, the lamp of hope burns on in this city's darkest haunts of vice.

More specious, yet not more solid, are the foundations on which a different class rest their hopes of eternal life. With a sort of general and indefinite trust in Christ, but without any humble, real, appropriating faith in his finished work and all-sufficient merits, your hopes, in the main, rest on what yourselves have done, or have not done, or intend to do. You are sober and chaste, — which many are not; you are honest men, or virtuous women; you bear an unblemished reputation; you have won the respect of the world; you maintain a reputable Christian profession; you are known by your charities; you say your prayers; you read your Bibles; you go to church; you attend the communion table. "These be thy gods, O Israel;" but, oh! wait till death comes, and if God have mercy on you at last, perhaps whether or no, you will turn to them to say, as said Job to his friends, Miserable comforters are ye all!

I do not deny that these hopes look bright; but so does the *ignis fatuus* that plays in the quagmire, luring the steps of the belated traveller to death. I grant that they yield bright visions; but so does the opiate which, while it pleases, poisons. Borne on their bosom your course is pleasant; but so is that of the boat which, with blue skies overhead, and beauty on either bank, is gliding on to the fatal cataract. From these hopes, if yours, I beseech you to turn to Christ,—" Turn you to the stronghold, ye prisoners of hope."

The hope of my text rests, not on the sinner's work, but on the Saviour's; on works, certainly, but not our own. God justifies none but those who condemn themselves, and loves none but those who, hating the works of the flesh, abhor themselves. Those only who have felt themselves lost, are found; nor are any pardoned but those who, putting in no plea but guilty, have cast themselves on the mercy of God through Jesus Christ our Lord. As the apostle says, it is "Christ in you, the hope of glory;" Christ on us in his righteousness, and in us in his image; enthroned in love on our hearts, and dwelling there by the indwelling of his Holy Spirit. Have you found him? Often offered, have you accepted him? Is it he whom your soul loveth? Have you laid the burden of your sins on his back, and your sick head on his bosom? Have you felt the beating of a new heart? and in new desires, new loves and hatreds, new aims and objects, can you say, Old things are passed away; behold, all things are become new? I congratulate you; the greatest kings might envy your condition. What though you are tossing on a sea of troubles, your anchor holds fast, having entered into that within the vail; and, to borrow an illustration which that well-known symbol suggests, some of you, old men if not old Christians, have not long now to lie off the harbour, exposed to the temptations and tossed on the storms of life—the hour comes when, having heaved your anchor and spread out your sails, you shall be borne safely over the swell that breaks on death's moaning bar, and pass into the haven of eternal rest.

> " Such are the hopes that cheer the just ;
> These hopes their God hath given ;
> His Spirit is the earnest now,
> And seals their souls for heaven."

III. Consider the certainty of this hope.

In that how different it is—

1. From such hopes of happiness as the world offers.

A fruit-tree in early summer, covered with a sheet of flowers, sounding with the hum of bees, topped by a thrush that pours forth a flood of song, standing on a sward enamelled with flowers and under calm blue skies that ring with music, offers a striking contrast to the same tree as it appears in autumn, with the ground around it strewed with withered leaves, and only a few fruits of all those rich blossoms hanging on its half-naked branches. Still greater the contrast between this world, as it presents itself to the eyes of youth, and as it appears to those of age. How rarely are its expectations of happiness fulfilled ! of its blossoms how few ever ripen into fruit ! It is common here for speakers and authors to summon two famous kings,—

the Jew, laying down the cup of all earthly pleasures to seize the pen, and write, Vanity of vanities, all is vanity; and the Greek, laying down the sword to weep, that having conquered one world he had not a second to conquer. Those crowned heads may be left undisturbed in their graves. Every man with gray hairs can tell as well as they, that this world, in whatever of its pleasures he has sought for happiness, is full of disappointment. How many parents, lovers, friends, have met bitter misery where they looked for joy! They indeed may be accounted fortunate who, merely disappointed, have not had their experience of the world foreshadowed by what befell St Paul, when from the fire at which he expected to warm his shivering limbs, a viper sprung to sting him. Without the hopes of my text, this world were vanity at its best; and how often also vexation of spirit?

2. From the hopes of the ungodly and unbelieving.

Who among us, asks Isaiah, shall dwell with the devouring fire? who among us shall dwell with everlasting burnings? Change the *shall* there into *will*, and I answer, None. As we have often seen and sought to prevent, the poor moth, allured by its glare, may, narrowing its circles, dash at length into the flame, and drop dead on our book; but such a fate, every sinner, however near to hell he ventures, intends and hopes to escape. He resolves on amendment, but not now—at some future date. Buoyed up with such hopes, and grown bold, he ventures further and deeper into sin, till he is lost, like the heedless boy who, borne up on his airy float, pushes out from the calm waters of the bank, further and deeper into the body of the current, and caught at length in its resistless sweep, is hurried down helpless and powerless into the fatal pool. They hope to amend, and never do; growing worse instead of better, dying as they lived. Be assured that, if it be true that as the tree falls so it lies, it is about as true that as the tree leans so it falls. A solemn fact! On you who are hesitating, hanging, halting between the two opinions—God or the world, Christ or pleasure, the indulgence of the flesh or the hopes of heaven—how should it enforce this saying, "Behold, now is the accepted time; behold, now is the day of salvation."

I am not charging you with hypocrisy. No. You do not profess to be religious, though you intend one day to be so; yet Job's description of the hopes of the hypocrite applies equally to yours—they are a spider's web. What more beautiful than those threads thrown from branch to branch of the golden gorse—an aerial bridge—all gemmed with diamonds of morning dew? But would any man in his senses trust his weight to it? And while, most false security, it snaps at an infant's touch, see how, crouching in the centre of her web, a cruel, cunning, bloody, venomous, ugly murderer sits, watching for her prey; and how over those silken strands lie scattered the wings and limbs, and disembowelled carcasses of once happy creatures, that shone in the gayest colours, and danced, all day long, in sunbeams. Equally ensnaring and insecure are the hopes of the unbelieving and ungodly, "whose hope," to use the words of Job, "shall be cut off, and whose trust shall be a spider's web. He shall lean upon his house, but it shall not stand; he shall hold it fast, but it shall not endure."

3. Now look at the certainty of the hope of my text.

I have a good security in the word of an honest man, still better in his bond, and, best of all, in his oath. On such an oath I will embark my fortune; I will believe the most extraordinary statements; sitting on a jury, I will hang a man—set him free, or send him to the gallows. If such certainty is afforded by the word of an honest, though fallen and sinful, man, what security is that which lies in the oath of God? So anxious is he, our heavenly Father, that poor sinners should believe that he will save them, is anxious to save them, has no more pleasure in your death and damnation than I would have in seeing my son die or damned, has given his own Son to save you, and will save you now if you will only come to him, that he has sworn it, passed his great oath for it—"Wherein God," says the apostle, "willing more abundantly to shew unto the heirs of promise the immutability of his counsel, confirmed it by an oath: that by two immutable things, in which it was impossible for God to lie, we might have a strong consolation, who have fled for refuge to lay hold upon the hope set before us : which hope we have as an anchor of the soul, both sure and steadfast." I can add nothing to that. To paint a rose, or gild the burnished gold, would be a less waste of time and labour than any attempt to augment the force of that. Heaven has no further security to offer; and if people will not believe the oath of God, I have nothing more to say.

As to those who rest on his word and oath, what hopes, what happiness like theirs! Now, said one, I can shake hands with death—Save Christ's, said another, no countenance to me so beautiful as death's! Enjoying this hope the believer may walk in perpetual sunlight, and go singing on his way to heaven. Under her eye how do all things change—sick-beds, losses, disappointments, bereavements? They throw their furnace-light on the face of Jesus, as sitting by the fire, a refiner, he purifies, not destroys his gold; and the death-struggle itself, with its tossings, and groans, and pains, appears as the effort of a bird to burst its shell, of the insect to shatter its case and enter on a new and bright existence. Looking on the grave as a bed for the weary, and as one from whose long and quiet sleep we shall rise, not as we do now, with the infirmities and weaknesses under which we lay down, but in the beauty of perfect holiness and the bloom of everlasting youth, there are times when Christian hope can use the words of Brainerd, My heart turns longing to the burying-place. Yes; we shall be happiest when our heads lie beneath the sod—we shall then be with the Lord; and, as surely as faith falls short of sight, we shall find that our brightest, dearest, loftiest hopes never rose to the height of our enjoyments— "Eye hath not seen, nor ear heard, neither have entered into the heart of man, the things which God hath prepared for them that love him." May these hopes draw us more and more heavenward; purify our hearts; wean our affections from earth, and wed them to the skies! May they help us to live above this world, and to look beyond it; and, as sailors, homeward bound, crowd every sail on the mast where the watch sits aloft looking out for land, may we, guided by the Spirit of God, inspired with the hopes of the gospel, and enabled to welcome such failings of nature as prognosticate the change at hand, haste, to use the words of Peter, be "hasting unto the coming of the day of God!" Then what?

> "The pains of death are past;
>   Labour and sorrow cease;
> And, life's long warfare closed at last,
>   The soul is found in peace.
> Soldier of Christ, well done;
>   Praise is thy new employ;
> And while eternal ages run,
>   Rest in thy Saviour's joy."

VII.

THE GRACE OF CHARITY.

"Now abideth charity;
The greatest of these is charity."— 1 COR. xiii. 13.

OUR version of the Bible, like the men who made it and those also who use it, is not faultless. It cannot be so, for "who can bring a clean thing out of an unclean?" The web must ever, more or less, partake of the imperfection of the loom. Still, the good and learned men to whom King James committed the work of translation, take it altogether, have done it well; so well, that all succeeding attempts to produce a better have failed. And perhaps the time and labour which some authors have spent in detecting and exposing the small faults of our version, would have been as well employed in correcting the large faults of their own creeds and conduct. Could I form a better wish than that the errors of our heart and life were as insignificant as those that have been detected in our English Bible; and that Christians, in their spirit and life, were as faithful copies of Jesus Christ, as it is of the divine original!

Beside those mistranslations which make our version somewhat erroneous, but which are hardly in any case of the smallest practical importance, a few passages of Scripture are liable to misunderstanding, in consequence of the change of meaning which some English words have undergone in the course of time. We have an example of this in the first chapter of St Paul's Epistle to the Romans. He says, "I would not have you ignorant, brethren, that oftentimes I purposed to come unto you, but was let hitherto." Now, *let*, in modern language, means permitted; but there, with its old meaning, it expresses the very opposite, *hindered*. And of such change, my text also affords a very striking example. Charity is a term now limited almost entirely to mean kindness bestowed on the poor. So by a charitable man, we understand one whose name is a household word in their homes; and who of his substance, be it great or small, gives liberally to feed the hungry, to clothe the naked, to instruct the ignorant, to house the homeless, and to supply the need of widows and orphans. This chapter itself proves that that application of the term does not exhaust, or at all come up to the meaning of the word as employed by Paul; for he supposes, as quite a possible case, a man who, though very charitable in the common sense of the term, is yet destitute of charity—declaring, "Though I bestow all my goods to feed the poor, and though I give my body to be burned, and have not charity, it profiteth me nothing." Before, therefore, setting forth some of those features of charity which led Paul to exalt her over all the other graces, awarding her the palm and crown, let us consider—

I. What we are to understand by charity.

It is an old word for love, that inner fountain of which kindness to the poor is but one of many streams; and where, when neither ruffled by passion nor polluted by sin, God, who is love, sees his own face, the reflection of his features, as we see ours on looking into a draw-well. I need not tell you who have been familiar with love from your earliest days what it is. At our birth she received us into her arms and welcomed us into the world. Love is associated with the first face our opening faculties recognised, with the first name our infant lips ever lisped, and with the pure, deep affection of one who pressed us, new born, to her happy bosom; and nursing us from the fountains of her breast, forgat all the world in the helpless creature cast upon her care. Flowing through the earth like streams amid desert sands, shining in life's darkest nights like stars in a wintry sky, throwing a bright bow over every cloud of fortune, to love, more than to anything else, this world owes what blessedness it enjoys. Life without it would not be worth the having; and without it, though we had a house, and that house a palace, we could not have a home.

Of this tenderest and strongest passion, what beautiful illustrations lie, shining like diamonds, in Bible story! In Rizpah, lone woman, who by seven gibbets guards the bodies of her sons, nor rises by night or day for weeks but to scare away the vulture or front the hungry wolf, love forgets herself—her only care the rotting dead. In Judah, yonder, she pleads for Benjamin, and offers, so he be set at liberty, to wear a brother's bonds. In that wronged though guilty mother, who, on seeing her babe in the hands of the executioner, raises a piercing shriek, and, casting herself at the king's feet, cries, O my lord, give her the living child, and in no wise slay it, love consents to part with her dearest object to save its life. Nay: in David, who, forgetting all Absalom's crimes at the news of his death, bursts into this cry of wildest, deepest grief, O my son Absalom! my son, my son Absalom! would God I had died for thee, O Absalom, my son, my son! love would buy another's life at the expense of her own. In the graves of the dead she buries all their crimes, and waters with her tears the memory of their virtues. In the garden where Peter sees his Lord betrayed, beset, and ready to be bound, she takes no count of numbers; but, casting prudence to the wind, rushes on the foremost foe, striking for her master. In Paul her hand trembles while she writes the doom of the ungodly, her eyes blot the page with tears, and she is willing to be herself accursed from Christ, so that countrymen and kindred are saved. One example more! You have anticipated it, and your thoughts, outrunning my words, have fixed on that amid whose transcendent glory these all are lost—like stars swallowed up in the blaze of day. Love, perfect, divine, hangs on the Cross of Calvary; and speaks in him who, turning an eye of pity on his bloody murderers, cries, Father, forgive them; for they know not what they do. Well may Paul say, Now abideth faith, hope, charity, these three; but the greatest of these is charity.

This love embraces not itself, but others—God, and all down from the throne of his majesty, to the lowest creatures of his hand. I have seen a plant with tendrils fitted to seize on any object within its reach, that, lying prostrate on the ground, had its leaves and flowers all soiled with mud, and its arms twined, and twisted, and tangled into each other—like a rope of many strands; and near by was another of the same species, with its arms flung lovingly around a tall and friendly tree, whose stem they held in close embrace, while they lent it, in return for its support, a robe of green leaves spangled all with flowers. Lying basely in its own embraces, the first was an image of selfishness; but in that which clothed and adorned the object to which it fondly clung, and from which no storm could tear its arms, I saw the love which, Queen of the Graces, "suffereth long, and is kind; seeketh not her own; beareth all things, believeth all things, hopeth all things, endureth all things."

II. Let us look at some of the features of this grace.

1. It is a power of universal influence. Many powers of nature are not always or everywhere in action. There are lands where rain, and others where snow never falls; rivers of water which no winter freezes, of ice which no summer melts. There is a metal which fire cannot burn; there is life which water cannot drown; and the lightning that flashes along a thousand miles of iron is stopped by a film of glass. Happily for the world, the destructive powers of nature are not always active. Etna and Heckla exhaust their forces, and long ages may pass ere they recover them for a new eruption. It is at rare intervals that earthquakes shake our globe, or the skies flash with lightnings, or hurricanes sweep through the troubled air, and lashing the sea into mountain billows, strew its shore with wrecks. Day leaves our world, and that light which paints its colours on every flower, and touches the clouds with gold, and wakes each morning the song of birds and hum of busy cities, departs with the setting sun. Winter ascends her throne, and waving an icy sceptre over fields and forests, stops all growth; once clothed in green, the trees are leafless; once enamelled with flowers, the meadows are bare. But the powers of winter in their turn cease; nature bursts her icy tomb; rising, she throws off her shroud of snow, while, their chains melted by the breath of spring, the streams, like

happy children set loose from the constraint of school, rush off, laughing, dancing, singing on their way to their home and parent in the deep.

But while substances, and places, and seasons limit the action of many material agencies, there is a power—that which England's greatest philosopher discovered—which neither substance, nor place, nor season limits. Universal in its action, it is everywhere, affecting everything. It determines the movements of the motes in a sunbeam, and of the planets in the firmament; it shapes the tear on your infant's cheek, and has given its rounded form to the sun; it makes the rain-drops fall to the earth, and prevents the stars from dropping out of the sky. Most powerfully affecting every atom of matter on earth, and every planet and sun in heaven, amid all the agencies which science studies, art employs, and God has established, gravitation alone extends its empire from the centre to the circumference of creation. In a subordinate sense, indeed, we may say of it what is said of God, It reigneth over all.

Now, such place Love holds in the kingdom of grace. In representing it as the ruling principle which should shape and influence all our conduct to God, in our families, to our friends, ay, and also to our foes, for, followers of him who died for his enemies, we are to love ours—blessing them which curse us, and praying for them which despitefully use us—I do not exaggerate its importance. Love was the dominant power in St Paul, and the principle of his whole obedience; "The love of Christ," he says, "constraineth us." And did not our Lord himself assign it such an imperial place? Those ten commandments from which all duties branch, like the boughs of a tree from the parent stem, he brings into the compass of a word, a single, simple word; that word—Love. Thou shalt love thy God, and Thou shalt love thy neighbour, are the whole duty of man. It is this that makes a religious, a happy life. With love, a dinner of herbs is better than a stalled ox; obedience is liberty with it; and without it slavery, call it by what name you may. And as it is earthly love, not its walls, however lofty, nor its furniture, however costly, nor its inmates, however great or beautiful, that makes a home below; so it is holy love that makes a heaven above, not its crowns, or palms, or harps, or robes; no, with reverence be it spoken, not God, or Christ, or saints, or angels, but love—their love. And as if by some strange power we could leave this nether world, and, winging our way upward, alight on a distant, starry sphere, we should find that we had not left that gravitation behind us, which binds all things and holds this world together; so saints shall find, on rising from the bed of death, and entering heaven, that they have but ascended into a region of purer and more perfect love.

"Faith, Hope, and Love now dwell on earth,
   And earth by them is blest;
But Faith and Hope must yield to Love,
   Of all the graces best.

The Grace of Charity.

"Hope shall to full fruition rise,
And Faith be sight above;
These are the means, but this the end,
For saints for ever love."

2. Love is a mighty power. Take Paul's description of it.

First, It "beareth all things." So I thought, on seeing a woman who presented a blessed and, though clad in rags, a beautiful contrast to those mothers who, committing most revolting murder, lay bloody hands on their new-born babes. To appearance she was one of those homeless creatures who are tossed about our city like the sea wrack that, torn by the rude storm from its native rocks, goes floating about the shore, washed in and washed out with each flowing tide. A threadbare shawl fell in scanty folds from her shoulders, and covered something held on her left arm. As, struck by her forlorn aspect, I was watching her movements, she suddenly stopped and raised the shawl. Then, as when a flood of golden sunlight, bursting through a rift in the clouds, and suddenly falling on some field, or hillside, or lake, or village, lightens up the scene, such change came over her face when she turned its earnest gaze on an infant that lay asleep, nestling in her bosom. You never saw a smile of more ineffable delight than this poor, perhaps guilty creature threw on her helpless charge. It was plain that she would have died for it—true to nature as the bear, who protects her young by offering her shaggy breast to the hunter's spear; and there, where love was turning what others might deem a burden into the one joy and blessing of the outcast's life, I thought of the words, it "beareth all things."

Second, It "believeth all things, hopeth all things." What will not parents bear from their children, and believe and hope of them? Did not Augustine's mother pray twenty long years for his conversion? And what is it but the hope that love breeds which still sustains the arms of praying fathers and mothers? You may quench the hopes of reason, but not those of love. It hopes against hope, and will soar like an eagle, which, rising with the rising tempest, mounts highest in stormy skies. Such hope sustained the mother, whom I saw intently gazing on the stone walls that immured·her boy. Opposite the prison gate, raised on the steps whence she could see the windows of the upper cells, her tall form clad in the attire of humble but honest life, and stooping under the burdens of grief and age, she stood, oblivious of all around, while her body went rocking to and fro with that swaying motion which bespeaks the deepest grief. An hour thereafter, rooted to the spot, there still she stood; her eyes, that swam in tears, and were fixed on an iron-barred window, telling as plainly as if her choking words had told it, that within those gloomy walls lay one that had once been cradled in her happy arms, and to whom, hoping all things, believing all things, her love yet clung, like ivy to a crumbling ruin.

The Grace of Charity.   119

Third, It "endureth all things." Take this example of that the last of those things which, according to Paul, love has the mind and also the might to do.

A ship, named the *Golden Gate*, takes fire some fifteen miles off the shores of America. Then rises a scene of the wildest and most terrible confusion. It is a battle now for life. Between the flames and the sea, it is every man for himself. While the roar of the fire, which rapidly gains on the fatal bark, is mingling with the prayers of some and the imprecations of others, a lady, with one child in her arms and another three years old at her knee, approaches the narrator of the story. I believe, she said, addressing him by name, that you are Mr Holloday? On being told that he was, she cried, Can you save my children? Madam, he replied, I do not know that I shall be able to save myself. Whereupon, pointing with a solemn air to the flames as they raged furiously in the centre of the ship, she exclaimed, Oh! if my children can be saved, I will consent to be burned in that fire!—they were saved, and she perished, an example of the might of love. It "endureth all things."

How should such cases of natural affection confirm God's people in their trust that he will not forget or forsake them; and others in their hopes that he will not refuse to forgive, but open wide his loving arms to every penitent, returning sinner! " Thus saith the Lord," speaking of his Church, " Behold, I will extend peace to her like a river, and the glory of the Gentiles like a flowing stream: then shall ye suck, ye shall be borne upon her sides, and be dandled upon her knees. As one whom his mother comforteth, so will I comfort you." What a depth is there in that love which God chooses as an image of his own! and yet the love of a mother's heart is but a drop from that illimitable ocean into which our sins, though great as mountains, once cast are lost for ever—buried out of sight. I believe that his love as far exceeds a mother's, when it is deepest and strongest, as does the strength of his almighty arm that of the infant which hangs helpless on her breast. She may forget—a fact which the blood of murdered infants proclaims, as, unheeded by a justice that wears her sword in vain in this guilty land, it cries aloud to heaven for vengeance: "yet," he says, "will I not forget thee. Behold, I have graven thee upon the palms of my hands."

Now, as it is by his love, seen in the face and form of a dying Saviour, that God melts the stony heart and subdues sinners to himself, so to this power also, under God, we must trust if we would bend stubborn wills, reclaim the vicious, and save the lost. The voice that grates harshly on the ear, the eye that does not glisten with tears but glares with anger, never made the bad good, or the good better. Men are not to be scolded into the love of God; nor can the terrors of hell frighten any into the love of heaven. Who would revive dead souls, let him learn his lesson in the chamber where the prophet, to restore the Shuna-

The Grace of Charity.

mite's son, rose from his knees, and took the boy into such loving, close embraces, that the heart of the living beat against the heart of the dead. Deal not with ungodly children, or careless and irreligious friends, without taking care to shew that you love the sinners as much at least as you hate their sins. Cultivate true, gentle, Christ-like love. What good may you not do, what stubborn hearts may you not melt, what hatred and hardness may you not subdue by the outgoings and expression of that love which is averse from censure but prone to praise; which pities while it blames; which, unselfish, "seeketh not her own;" which touches wounds with a tender hand; and which, ready to cover a multitude of sins, spake through him who, purest of the pure, and holiest of the holy, said, as he looked with pity on the guilty woman, Neither do I condemn thee: go, and sin no more?

3. Love is the grand principle of the gospel.

A child had strayed from its mother's side, and, gathering buttercups and daisies, had approached the edge of a precipice. On raising her head, what was the mother's horror to see her darling tottering on the dreadful brink! If she cries, alarmed or in gleesome play, he takes another backward step, and perishes. With prompt, instinctive wisdom, though with trembling hands, she bares her bosom; and caught, to use St Paul's words, by guile, the infant, seeking its accustomed pleasure, runs into her arms. She saved her child by addressing its self-love. And so also was one saved who, where a bridge thrown from rock to rock spans a yawning chasm, was wont to lie over watching the waters that, ground into snowy foam, rushed, and whirled, and roared below. A servant found the urchin on his way from school hanging over the dizzy ledge, and so absorbed in the strange pleasure as not to notice the other's approach. Clutching him, as the hawk her prey, he seized the boy, and raising, held him out for a moment at arm's length over the brink of death. The dreadful experiment had the desired effect. The fright cured him; and, indeed, when that boy had grown into a man he used to tell that he never passed the place without recollections that made him shudder.

Now, dealing with us not as angels, which we are not, not as unfallen, but as sinful, disobedient, headstrong, and foolish children, God does employ means like these. He addresses himself to our self-love—to our taste for pleasure, and our dread of pain. Unwilling that any should perish, like a father or mother in such circumstances, he loves us too well to leave any argument untried; therefore heaven has been revealed, that its palms, and crowns, and thrones, might draw us to God; and the pit also has opened, that the worm that never dieth, and the flames that are never quenched, and poor wretches gnawing their tongues and gnashing their teeth might scare away the thoughtless and turn them from the paths of sin. Therefore Jesus also, lover of our souls, presents salvation in the form of a matter of profit and loss. Making such an appeal as does a father who implores his son, if he will not regard his father's and mother's feelings, to look to his own interests, and think of the misery and ruin which his sins and follies will bring on himself, Jesus asks, and I would urge you all to consider and answer the question, "What shall it profit a man, if he shall gain the whole world, and lose his own soul?" Therefore God also puts these solemn, awful questions, "Who among us shall dwell with the devouring fire? who among us shall dwell with everlasting burnings?" Would God men would look these questions in the face, and flee to Christ's open arms, hasting from the wrath to come—nor long, perhaps, to come! There is but a step between us and the grave.

There is a fable of a tree, which, as it fell groaning to the earth, discovered that out of its own timber the woodman had hafted the axe which entered its heart and felled it to the ground; and there is another of an eagle that, pierced by an arrow as it soared in the skies, discerned, while it lay dying on the ground, that its own wing had furnished a feather to the shaft that drank up its blood. Well, sceptics, abandoning the weapons with which Hume, Gibbon, Tom Paine, and Voltaire vainly attempted to overthrow our faith, have thought to find in the Bible itself that which would feather their arrow or haft their axe. Because the Bible, in addressing itself to our self-love, appeals to the lowest principle of our nature, it cannot, they say, be divine. An objection this that only proves the darkness of their understandings, or the malignity of their hearts! Restrained within proper bounds, self-love is a right feeling; one that, divinely implanted, is not a vice but a virtue which—winning the drunkard, for example, to practise sobriety and respect himself—would gladden many a wretched home.

Nor is it to this only, or chiefly, that our heavenly Father appeals. Take the apostle Paul as a type of the Christian! His strongest passion was the love of Christ. Gratitude for his salvation, affection for his person, admiration of his character, regard to his will and honour, his crown and kingdom, these constrained him to love, not himself, but him who died for him and rose again. And what motive nobler, tenderer, than that love to God, to Christ, to saints, to sinners, to friends, to foes, under the influence of which all come on entering into a state of grace. In leaving sin we leave selfishness; the less sinful we become, in that very proportion we become the less selfish. The whole case is related in the story of the prodigal. The pangs of hunger, his shame, his ragged misery, death in prospect, with no gentle forms by his side, or kind hands to wipe his brow, and close his eyes, and give his poor body decent burial, these troubles, no doubt, turned his thoughts homeward, and, blessed of God, led to the reflection, "How many hired servants of my father's have bread enough and to spare, and I perish with hunger! I will arise and go to my father, and will say unto him, Father, I have sinned against heaven, and before thee, and am no more worthy to be called thy son: make me as one of thy hired servants." As ships run before the storm to anchor-ground and sheltering bay, he made for home, if I may say so, through stress of weather; and, as when the tempest-tossed have reached the desired haven, how sweet the change—fatted calf for swinish husks, that goodly robe for rags, the flowing bowl, and merry music, and gay dancers for the neglect and wretchedness to which his harlots and boon companions had left him —first their slave, and then their victim! Yet it was not these home-pleasures that kept him there; but love for that loving father, who, forgiving all, had folded him to his bosom, and bathed his face with tears of overflowing joy, and, glad to have a long-lost son restored, had assembled the neighbours to share his happiness; for the grave had given up its prey—he that was dead was alive again, he that had been lost was found.

Love is the chain that binds us to the throne of God, each to all and all to each. May its golden links be strengthened! Gift to be coveted above all others, rather than eloquence lofty as angels' speech, than power to pluck mountains from their roots and cast them into the boiling sea, than knowledge that penetrates into the deepest mysteries and climbs to the heights of heaven, than the courage that wins the martyr's crown at a burning stake, than the faith that tramples death beneath its feet, than the hope that, stretched on a dying bed lays a mortal hand on an immortal crown, rather far than these, give me the love that dwells, dove-like, in many a lowly bosom, and turns the rudest cabin into a little heaven. "Now abideth faith, hope, charity, these three; but the greatest of these is charity." St Paul crowns her queen; and so I say, with this apostle elsewhere, Put on therefore, as the elect of God, holy and beloved, bowels of mercies, kindness, humbleness of mind, meekness, long-suffering; forbearing one another, and forgiving one another. . . . . And above all these things, put on charity, which is the bond of perfectness.

VIII.

THE GOOD FIGHT.

"I have fought a good fight."—2 TIM. iv. 7.

"THE gods do so unto me, and more also, if the dust of Samaria shall suffice for handfuls for all the people that follow me." Such insolent message did Ben-hadad send to the king of Israel. Ahab's reply was as spirited as it was wise, and one that, from such a man as the husband of Jezebel, and the cowardly murderer of Naboth, was like the fire that flashes, when it is struck, from a cold, black flint; "Tell him," said the king, roused by the insult, and perhaps inspired for the occasion, "Let not him that girdeth on his harness boast himself as he that putteth it off." Prophetic words! Ere four-and-twenty hours the Syrian host was scattered by the arms, or, rather, by the God of Israel, like autumn leaves before the wind; and this proud boaster, foremost of a band of horsemen, was galloping away for life.

When the apostle, the humblest as well as the holiest of men, used the words from which I intend to speak, he did not lie open to any such taunt as Ahab's. He was no young disciple on his way to battle with armour unsoiled and arm unwearied. Nor, like many a Christian man, was he in the thick of it, now giving and now receiving blows; now with sword flashing and voice shouting, pressing forward, and now, alas! borne back; now brought to his knees, and again, rescued by his captain and revived by prayer, rising to his feet to rush on his foes and renew the combat. Paul was in none of these circumstances. He had reached the close of a long warfare. In him we behold a veteran great in fight and gray in years. On his arm a battered shield; his hand returning to its scabbard a sword that had been often buried in the body of his sins; on his head the helmet of salvation, dinted with the blows of many a hard-fought fight; he stands before us—covered, if I may say so, with the scars of a hundred battles, and crowned with the laurels of a hundred victories. His sufferings, toils, trials, travels, preachings, prayings over, with foot planted on the threshold of glory, he is about to enter on his reward. The battle fought, the victory won, nothing remains but to die—and that he accounted nothing. The dark valley, in fear of which so many are all their lifetime subject to bondage, dreading it as the hardest part of the course, he does not reckon as else than the goal by which the racer stands, panting, to receive the crown; he says, "I have finished my course." Nor does he regard death as his enemy; not he. He has no quarrel with death; no fear of it; no battle to fight with it; "I have fought a good fight," he says—fought it out. It is done and over; and never were silent night and soft couch more welcome at the close of a long day's journey or of a hard day's fighting, than death and the grave to him who exclaimed, "I am now ready to be offered, and the time of my departure is at hand. I have fought a good fight, I have finished my course, I have kept the faith: henceforth there is laid up for me a crown of righteousness, which the Lord, the righteous judge, shall give me at that day: and not to me only, but unto all them also who love his appearing."

I. Look at the Christian life under the aspect of a fight.

In a sense, this aspect of life is not peculiar to that of the Christian's. Look at the world! What a scene of disquiet and disorder! what a succession of struggles, which many begin at the cradle and leave not but at the grave! With poverty, or hard toil, or disease, or domestic trials, or unavoidable misfortunes, or, in some cases, all of these together, many have to battle their whole way through life—they rise up early, and lie down late, and eat the bread of sorrow. How does ambition, not confined to any class, spur on the eager competitors in the race for honours or riches! What a struggle there is amongst the different members of society to get uppermost! and while some are straining every nerve to improve their position, it needs the utmost endeavours of others to keep theirs.

How like this world often seems to a rock at sea, on which, eager to escape the jaws of death, more drowning men seek standing-room than it offers; and when they whose gain has been others' loss, when the few that have risen on the shoulders of the many that sink, have possessed themselves in wealth, or power, or pleasure, of the objects of their ambition, they have only reached a bare, black, unsheltered rock, on which, at some future day, a giant wave rises roaring to sweep them from their slippery footing. Let no man deceive himself. Even this world is not to be got without fighting; and, compared with the nobler struggles and prizes of the faith, though its rewards be laurel or even golden crowns, it presents a scene of no more real dignity than a nursery quarrel— children fighting for some gilded toy—the street where ragged boys struggle, and tear, and roll over each other for a few copper coins. I admit that it has pleasures; but its sweetest enjoyments perish in the using. I admit that it has roses; but they are beset with thorns, and the hand that plucks them bleeds. Nor are any of these to be obtained without a struggle. The few prizes which, among many blanks, the world offers to a host of competitors are won only by the hard work, hard struggling, hard fighting, without which you gain no topmost place in any profession, no heaps of money, no niche in the temple of fame. Its pearls are not to be picked up among the pebbles of the shore; he who would possess, must seek them in a sea where sharks are swimming and storms rage. Indeed, I dare to say that, so far from the followers of the world being exempt from toil and hardship, it would not take a man half the care and time and trouble to get to heaven, which it takes any man to get rich, and many a man to get to hell. The question, therefore, is not whether we shall fight, but what for, and on whose side?—on that of Jesus, whose award is life, or on that of sin, whose wages is death?

Now, with regard to the Christian's fight, I remark,
1. He has to fight against the world.

It hated me, says our Lord, before it hated you. It had no crown for his brow but one of thorns; it found no way to exalt him but on a bloody cross; and when he, at whose approach happy angels threw open the gates of heaven, appeared at its door, it refused him a night's lodging. The foxes have holes, was his complaint, and the birds of the air have nests; but the Son of man hath not where to lay his head. And if there was a time when Jerusalem poured forth her exultant thousands to escort her king to his capital, this popularity was but such a fitful gleam as I have seen light up a cold and stormy day. The servant is no better than his master; and I do believe, were we more true to God, more faithful and honest in opposing the world for its good, we should get less smoothly along the path of life, and have less reason to read with apprehension these words of Jesus, Woe unto you, when all men shall speak well of you. Not less true than shrewd was the remark of a Scotchwoman respecting one who, just settled in the ministry, had been borne to his pulpit amid the plaudits of all the people,—If he is a faithful servant of the Lord Jesus Christ, he will have all the blackguards in the parish on his head before a month is gone.

I am not saying that the world is always wrong in its judgments, or that it is always right to go against its customs. Alas! the children of this world are sometimes wiser in their generation than the children of light. But, as a living fish is often found cleaving its way against the stream, and that fish is certainly dead which, floating on the top, is always moving with it, so he is no living Christian whom you ever find walking according to the course of this world. They who would wear a crown in heaven must be ready to oppose its maxims, to encounter its offence, to brave its opposition, to scorn its contempt, and to sacrifice to its friendships as well as to resist its allurements. "Be not conformed to this world: but be ye transformed by the renewing of your mind," says this same apostle. Nor is that easy. Alas! how often do Christians follow a multitude to do evil; yield to the customs of the world because they are afraid of being thought singular; and fail in their duty because they are afraid of giving others offence! Few are bold for Christ, and dare avow themselves before the worldly, not ashamed of his cause, and cross, and crown. Bad men glory in their shame, and it would seem as if good men were ashamed of their glory. It ought not so to be. In the strength of God, then, stand up for the good, the holy, and the true; seeking men's profit, not their praise; pitying the world, though your reward here should be none else than his, who, finding a serpent frozen, warmed it in his bosom, to have it sting him for his pains. Be not discouraged by this, as if some strange thing had happened unto you. The servant is no better than his master, nor the disciple than his Lord.

2. He has to fight against Satan.

When Napoleon Buonaparte, watching the fortunes of the battle, saw the charge of our Scots Greys at Waterloo, as, launched on his columns, they dashed like a thunderbolt into the thick of them, crushing and bearing down all before them, he exclaimed, How terrible are these Greys! But what mortal foe so terrible as him we have to fight?—so relentless, so malignant, ever walking about seeking whom he may devour. No serpent so cunning, no roaring lion so savage! From other enemies escape may be found, from him none. Neither the world, nor the Church itself, offers any asylum, nor the universe, other than the hollow of God's hand, the shadow of his wings. Flying from the world, the hermit has courted solitude among the heights of the mountain, or in the depths of the gloomy forest; but, tracking his steps far from the haunts of men, in the desert region, where he was conquered by the Master, the Devil has often tempted and triumphed over the servant.

The Sabbath proclaims its weekly and welcome truce, a breathing time to such as have the temptations of the world's gaiety and the cares of its business to contend with; but Satan keeps no Sabbath,—he takes no rest, and gives none. More persuasive than the most eloquent preachers, and more wakeful than the most anxious hearers, if on holy Sabbaths, in sinners converted, in careless ones roused, in the perishing plucked from destruction, he sustains his greatest defeats, on those days he wins his most signal triumphs. Pardon is freely offered to the guilty, salvation to the lost, but, listening to him, they refuse to be saved; as never happened on the stormy ocean, they see the lifeboat leave them, straightway to resume their dance on the sinking wreck—Christ is rejected, warnings are despised. And, hardening the heart, not against the pleadings of a man, but the tears of divine pity and the very blood of Christ, Satan marches off thousands from the doors of the house of God, unconverted, unsaved, harder than they came in, to resume their way on the broad path that leadeth down to destruction.

Men have taken up arms against the greatest odds; and fighting on their own thresholds, with wives and children at their back, bleeding patriots have wrung victory from superior numbers. But, suppose a foe able to make themselves invisible; able to pass in a moment over leagues of country; able to live without sleep, to march without wearying, to work without food; who seldom fought but to conquer, and though repulsed often, were never destroyed; who pitied none, spared none; and regarding neither sex, nor innocence, nor age, dragged off their unhappy captives to horrible and nameless tortures—who would take the field against these? Such an enemy has no place in the pages and horrid annals of war; nor did man ever find such a foe in man. True, but he has such a foe in Satan. That you do not see him is nothing; you never saw the pestilence which it is death to breathe. That you do not see him makes him not the less, but all the more formidable. Victory over a foe like this I could neither expect nor dream of, but for such promises as these: " Fear not, thou worm Jacob, and ye men of Israel; I will help thee, saith the Lord, and thy Redeemer, the Holy One of Israel:" "How should one chase a thousand, and two put ten thousand to flight, except their Rock had sold them, and the Lord had shut them up?" "Thou shalt tread upon the lion and adder: the young lion and the dragon shalt thou trample under feet:" "Fear thou not, for I am with thee: be not dismayed, for I am thy God: I will strengthen thee; yea, I will help thee; yea, I will uphold thee with the right hand of my righteousness." Courage! A little child with God at his back, is mightier than the devil and all his angels. He that is with us is greater than all that be against us.

3. He has to fight against the flesh.

"The prince of this world cometh," said our Lord, "and hath nothing in me." Can we say so? Assuredly not. Hence the disadvantages under which we carry on the combat. He hath much in us, having in our natural depravity a traitor inside the gates, an ally to open the door and admit the enemy. Called, with such a nature, to contend both against the influences of a world that lieth in wickedness and the temptations of the Evil One, we sail, as it were, in a poor, crazy, damaged, leaking bark which has both wind and tide against her; nor is it any wonder that in circumstances so untoward multitudes make shipwreck of the faith. The wonder is, not that many never reach the harbour, but that any do—entering heaven as once I saw a vessel gain yonder port, bows crushed, masts sprung, and bulwarks gone; saved, but almost lost. And if the righteous scarcely be saved, where shall the ungodly and the sinner appear?

The prince of this world cometh, says our Saviour, and hath nothing in me; and so his temptations fell into Christ's bosom like flaming darts into the sea—hissing, but instantly quenched. It is otherwise, alas! with us. Our corrupt nature is food for temptation, as flax is food for flame; we are ready "to be set on fire of hell." And with such natural dispositions, the marvel is, not that we sometimes fall into sin, but that we ever withstand. Satan had no corruption to work upon in his fellow-angels, yet he triumphed over their loyalty; and with one sweep of his dragon tail cast down perhaps a third part of the stars of heaven. He had no innate depravity to work upon in our first parents, yet again he triumphed, seducing the innocence of Eden. And to whom but God shall we ascribe the glory of this, that in yon Christian resisting the devil till he flee, earth stands fast, where heaven fell; and faith conquers, where innocence was defeated, — in the words of Scripture, and the spiritual history of many, "the lame take the prey." Like Samson, who made a greater slaughter of the Philistines after his locks were shorn, than he had ever done when they fell flowing over his ample shoulders, man achieves a greater triumph after his fall than he did before it. Such is the power of imparted and omnipotent grace! He giveth power to the faint; and to them that have no might he increaseth strength; and thus God makes all things work for his glory—the wrath of devils, as well as of men, to praise him.

II. The character of the Christian's fight; it is "a good fight."

1. Because it is in a good cause.

With the justice and reason of any war, our soldiers are supposed to have nothing to do; these are to be discussed in Parliament, but not in barrack-rooms. The theory of a standing army is such, that from the commander-in-chief down to the drummer-boy, the soldier is considered as much a mere machine as the musket in his hands. This presents to many, one of the most serious and difficult questions as to the lawfulness of his profession. While we may feel no such scruples, it ought to make us, as far as possible, live peaceably with all men, and never but as a last resort appeal to the arbitrament of arms. How often have good men been found fighting on the bad side! and how often has the trumpet summoned from their distant homes and peaceful occupations, those who had no quarrels to settle, nor wrongs to complain of, to the bloody work of slaughter ; to destroy each other's lives and to mangle each other's bodies, till, in that poor, mutilated humanity, a mother would not know her own son! In war both sides cannot be right ; and the death of every man, therefore, who falls on the side that stands up for the right against the wrong is a murder, on which the Almighty Judge will hold severe and solemn inquest—laying the guilt at the right door. But, however soldiers may come to regard themselves, or be regarded by others, as machines who are to obey orders without inquiring into the merits of the war, still a man is a man—he has what his arms have not, reason and conscience ; nor can he, though he would, suppress their voice within him. I can fancy cases where he has little heart to fight. He is not sure that it is " a good fight." Ordered to cut down one, who, though a naked savage, stands on the shore of his country to defend it from aggressors, or on the threshold of his door to protect his wife and daughters from the hands of a brutal soldiery, the sympathies of a generous man cannot be on the same side as his sword.

Now, if, soldiers of the Cross, you have formidable enemies to contend with, you have an immense advantage in this—that your cause is just, and noble, and holy, and good. It is "a good fight." Your enemies are not your kindred, bone of your bone, flesh of your flesh; they are the enemies of God and Christ; of virtue and liberty: of light and peace; of your children and of your race; of your bodies and of your souls— tyrants that would bind you in chains worse than iron, and burn, not your house above your head, but yourself in hell for ever. I am not saying that the sword has not often flashed on the side of right and been bathed in tyrants' blood; but men never drew sword in a cause like this; nor to any battle so much as that to which I summon you with the world, the devil, and the flesh, are the few pithy words of a brave old general so appropriate. His men were waiting to be addressed ere the fight began. Erect in his saddle, with his gray hairs streaming in the wind, he stretched out his arm, and pointing to the foe in front said, ere he rang out the word Fire! There are the enemy; if you do not kill them, they will kill you. So with us. We must destroy sin, or be destroyed by it. Be assured that unless your prayers stop your sins, your sins will stop your prayers; and that by God's help you must kill sin, or sin will kill you.

2. Because here victory is unmingled joy.

It is not so in other fights. The laurels that are won where groans of suffering mingle with the shouts of battle, are steeped in tears; and when cannon roar and bells ring out a victory, and shouting crowds throng the streets, and illuminations turn night into day, dark is many a home, where fathers and mothers, brothers and sisters, widows and orphans, weep for the brave who shall never return. It is said of God, that, in sweet flowers, and singing birds, and painted shells, and shining stars, in all the beautiful and happy works of his hands, he takes delight; but the best and bravest soldiers have sickened at the sight of the work of their hands in that field of carnage where, locked like brothers in each other's arms, friend and foe lie quietly together in one gory bed. There are thorns in victory's proudest crown. He whom men called the Iron Duke, is reported to have said that there was nothing so dreadful as a battle won, but a battle lost.

Thank God, our joy over sins slain, bad passions subdued, Satan defeated, has to suffer no such abatements. Heaven, that I can fancy hiding its eyes from other battles, watches the fortunes of this with keenest, and kindest interest; angels rejoice in your success; nor are any tears shed here but such as poured from the father's eye, when, kissing the returned prodigal and folding him in his happy embraces, he cried, Let us eat, and be merry: for this my son was dead, and is alive again; he was lost, and is found.

I wish to enlist you as soldiers of the Cross. This is a good fight in other than these, in all its aspects: what a captain in Jesus; what arms in the whole armour of God—the very ring and sight of which, as they shine in the beams of the Sun of righteousness, make Satan tremble; what a helmet for the head in salvation; what a shield in faith; what a breastplate in the righteousness that protects the believer's heart; what a sword in that of the Spirit, the word of God; what a girdle for the body in truth; in peace what shoes for the feet; and last of all, in a crown immortal, what a prize to reward your watchings and prayers, your tears and toils, the blows you strike and wounds you suffer! I can understand men in that terrible war which is now raging beyond the Atlantic, flying, as they are said to do, not through cowardice, but to escape military service. So long as the battle-cry is the Union *with* slavery, not *without* it, to me the ground of battle is not clear; I cannot feel, to use the words of my text, that it is "a good fight." But who can doubt that here? It is a fight for your soul; it is a battle for heaven; it is bleeding slaves up in arms against their old masters; doomed prisoners fighting their way to the open door, and dashing themselves on those who would bar their escape to life and liberty. Break away from your sins; and, taking unto you the whole armour of God, throw yourselves into this battle. By that I cannot say you will win heaven, but you will win to it; and thus possess the prize which your Saviour purchased.

No doubt it is a hard fight; I do not conceal or disguise that. How can it be easy for a man to overcome the world and crucify his own flesh? But if that is hard, it is harder far to suffer the pains of a lost soul, to lie down in everlasting burnings. Oh! surely better lose a hand, than have the whole body burn; better part with some darling sin than part with Jesus. You have no choice; they only that carry swords on earth shall wave palms in heaven; nor shall any but they who walk here in armour, walk there in brightness. The crown is for saints, not for sinners; not for cowards, but for conquerors. And how can you conquer unless you fight? The promises are to him that conquers, to him that overcometh, — not, indeed, by might, nor by power, but by my spirit, saith the Lord of hosts,—" To him that overcometh will I give to eat of the tree of life, which is in the midst of the paradise of God;" "He that overcometh shall not be hurt of the second death;" "He that overcometh, the same shall be clothed in white raiment; and I will not blot out his name out of the book of life, but I will confess his name before my Father, and before his angels;" and still higher honour, "To him that overcometh will I grant to sit with me in my throne."

IX.

THE TRIAL AND TRIUMPH OF FAITH.

"Arise, get thee to Zarephath, which belongeth to Zidon, and dwell there: behold, I have commanded a widow woman there to sustain thee."—1 KINGS xvii. 9.

THE plough is fatal to the picturesque. A country under husbandry, with its farms and formal divisions, each field throughout its whole extent of the same crop and colour, with all God's beautiful flowers cut down and cast out under the name of weeds, is as inferior in point of beauty as it is superior in point of profit to moor or mountain. How tame your levelled fields of wheat or barley compared with the rudest hill-side, where green bracken, and the plumes of the fern, and the bells of the foxglove, and brown heath with its purple blossoms, and the hoar, gray, rugged stones that lie scattered in wild confusion, unite to form a mantle, in richness and variety of hues, such as loom never wove and queen never wore. This variety should minister to more than taste. A pious mind, extracting food for devotion from the flowers which supply honey to the bee, finds profit where others find only pleasure, and, rising from nature up to nature's God, exclaims with David, O Lord, how manifold are thy works! in wisdom hast thou made them all!

Without this variety, how tame our gardens with every flower in form and colour the counterpart of another; and how monotonous the music of early morn did every lark in the sky, linnet in the bush, rook and ringdove in the woods, all utter the same notes! But variety characterises every department of nature. Each lamb of the flock has a bleat known to its own mother; each rose on the bush has its own shape and shade of colour; and there is not a lark that hangs carolling in the clouds but has a voice recognised by the brood above whose grassy nest she sings her morning hymn, calling the drowsy world to rise for worship and for work. Nor is this variety anywhere more remarkable than in mankind. It is calculated that there are ten hundred millions of our race scattered over the five continents and countless islands of the globe. Now, while in their grand characteristics, in their features, organs, voices, limbs, and general form these all resemble each other, yet there are not two faces, for instance, out of these ten hundred millions, which are exactly alike. Nor does a rich, boundless, divine variety characterise and adorn only this world of ours in the living creatures of its lands and seas, the shells which strew its shores, the flowers and fruits of its fertile plains, its shaggy mountains, up to their snowy crests. It shines above us—in stars fixed or moving, stars single, stars in pairs, stars in clusters, some sparkling with borrowed, others with native light; in the sun that runs his daily round, and comets, that with fiery locks streaming out behind them rush away into darkness, nor return for a hundred, perhaps for a thousand years. And high above that starry firmament, amid the splendours of the upper sanctuary, in angels and archangels, in cherubim and seraphim, in saints on higher thrones and crowns of brighter glory, in the various orders of unfallen and the various honours of ransomed spirits, we see a manifold and magnificent diversity in the works of God.

From this we might conclude that the kingdom of grace would present something of the same variety as that which distinguishes all his other works; and that as neither all angels nor all insects are formed alike, no more would all Christians be so. And thus it is; for variety is one of the many points at which the kingdoms of grace and nature touch. Christians have individual peculiarities which, as much as their faces, distinguish them from each other; and this is rather a beauty than a blemish—a charm rather than a fault. Some have one grace and some another, in such prominence, that John's love, and Peter's ardour, and Paul's zeal, and Job's patience, and Moses' meekness, and Jeremiah's tenderness, and Abraham's faith, have become proverbial. Nor is this variety, as among the flowers of moor and meadow, an element merely of beauty. It is a power; an element of the highest utility in the Church. Hence the mistake of those who would have all Christians modelled on their own pattern, as, for example, of some modest, retiring, gentle spirits, who cannot appreciate the worth and usefulness of those whom God has cast in a rough mould and made of stern stuff.

In the early ages of the Church, when she is endowed with supernatural powers, and some have the gift of wisdom, others of knowledge, others of faith, others of healing, others of miracles, others of prophecy, others of tongues, others of interpretation, Paul by a beautiful analogy recommends mutual respect—illustrating the advantages of variety, and shewing how people with very different gifts may nevertheless be true members of Christ's true Church. "If the foot," he says, "shall say, Because I am not the hand, I am not of the body; is it therefore not of the body? And if the ear shall say, Because I am not the eye, I am not of the body; is it therefore not of the body? If the whole body were an eye, where were the hearing? If the whole were hearing, where were the smelling? But now God hath set the members every one of them in the body, as it hath pleased him. And if they were all one member, where were the body? But now are they many members, yet but one body. And the eye cannot say unto the hand, I have no need of thee: nor again, the head to the feet, I have no need of you." We live in an age of ordinary gifts; but it is as true of these ordinary as of those extraordinary gifts of the

Spirit, that there is as much utility as beauty in the diverse temperaments and endowments of Christian men. What is diverse is not of necessity adverse. God has different kinds of work to do; and since he chooses to employ men, he has need of different kinds of instruments.

I. In what is recorded of Elijah, he appears as one specially fitted for his work.

Go into the workshop of a mechanic; what a variety of tools is there! Some are straight, others crooked; some are blunt, others sharp as a razor; some are rough, others have the polish of a mirror; some are soft as silk, others hard as steel; some are light enough to be the playthings of his children, while it needs his own brawny arm to swing the ponderous weight of others. He finds a use for them all; nor can he dispense with any. Now, to compare great things with small, God's work to ours, it is by a corresponding diversity of accomplishments, and gifts, and dispositions in her members and ministers that the Church is thoroughly furnished for every good work. It had fared ill, for instance, with the cause of truth at the Reformation, if the gentleness of Philip Melancthon, however much we may admire it and love him, had not been associated with the rough and ready energy of Martin Luther. Knox, our own great Reformer, has been severely handled for his lack of courtly urbanity to Mary, and called rude, a brute, a rugged savage. But, as he himself said, when, having thwarted the Queen in her attempt to reimpose the hateful yoke of Popery on our land, he left her in tears, and was reproached, as he passed from the council chamber, for his rudeness, Better that women weep than bearded men! Of this heroic man we say what the Irish Presbyterian said, when asked beside the ruins of an old castle which the Protector had assailed with fire and sword, what he thought of Oliver Cromwell, he replied, God gave him stern work to do, and he did it! Knox was not more stern or rugged than the time required. Rugged? Who quarrels with the ruggedness of the rock that presents a bold front to the roaring sea, and, withstanding their shock, flings back the proud waves into their bed; defending the land from deluge, and its inhabitants from death? The times, it is said, make men. True; but it is as true that men are made for the times—raised up by God with gifts and graces suited to the work they have to do.

Of these remarks the illustrious man whose life supplies the incident recorded in my text, is a remarkable illustration. Elijah's lot was cast in evil and stormy days; and with his bold and dauntless spirit, how well was he fitted to face the dangers, and conquer the difficulties he had to encounter? The times called for a Boanerges, a son of Thunder; and, raised up by God, Elijah, stern in aspect and wild in dress, appears on the scene—rushing on the stage with a curse on his lips, and leaving it for heaven in a whirlwind and chariot of fire. He pronounced a doom of drought on the guilty land,—skies that should shut up their treasures, and yield neither dew nor rain ; and it was in consequence of this, that he was placed in the circumstances which the text brings before us. Directed by God, he fled for protection from the vengeance of Ahab to the lonely banks of Cherith, where the brook gave him drink, and the ravens brought him meat, as day by day, he whiled away the time, and woke the echoes of the rocks with the songs of David, singing,

> "The Lord's my shepherd, I'll not want.
> He makes me down to lie
> In pastures green : he leadeth me
> The quiet waters by."

Steering on black wing through the hot and stagnant air, the ravens supply his morning and evening meals ; and laying them at his feet, those caterers go to croak and whet their beaks on the overhanging trees—like servants who wait to satisfy their own wants with the fragments of their master's feast. Thus, by a singular miracle, did God answer his prayers, and give him day by day his daily bread. But at length, no dew falling from clear nor rain from cloudy skies, Cherith's stream begins to fail; each day its gurgling sound grows more and more faint; betimes it contracts to a tiny rill; at length it vanishes, leaving nothing in its bed but a course of dry, white stones. Now it is that God, who watched over his servant, says, Arise, get thee to Zarephath, which belongeth to Zidon, and dwell there: behold, I have commanded a widow woman there to sustain thee.

II. Consider the trial to which this put the prophet's faith.

1. He is sent for safety to a heathen city.

Unlike Moses, Samuel, David, for whose future greatness their previous history prepares us, as does the gray dawn for the full blaze of day, Elijah bursts on our notice. His appearance as a prophet of the most high God startles us not less by its suddenness than by its terror; how much more the weak and wicked Ahab that day, when, stalking into the palace in uncourtly robes, his shaggy raiment bound by a leathern belt, his aspect severe and stern, he walks up boldly to the king, and fixing his eye on him, says, "As the Lord God of Israel liveth, before whom I stand, there shall not be dew nor rain these years, but according to my word"—and so saying, vanishes. As the words of Christ which blasted the fig-tree—that emblem of formal Christians, these went forth like a poisonous breath, withering all vegetation in the guilty land. Gaunt famine came, but no repentance with it; only death, and deeper exasperation against the servant of God. No wonder, therefore, when the brook fails, that Elijah is not sent back to Ahab and the land of Israel. But God might have sent him to

Judah? True; and I can fancy the welcome and ovation he would have received from those who, unlike their kindred in Israel, clung to the temple and worship of their fathers' God. It does seem strange that, for protection from the dangers to which his opposition to idolatry had exposed him, he is sent, not to Judah, but to Zidon and Zarephath; to a land and city of idolaters. Like a man who has got out of his depth, and, drowning, turns his back on the shore and his face to the sea, was not this but making bad worse? It was as if one flying in terror from a lion, was directed to seek refuge in the lion's den.

I conferred not, says St Paul, with flesh and blood. Had he done so, he had never, counting all things loss for Christ, become the great apostle of the Gentiles; had Moses done so, he had never, esteeming the reproach of Christ greater riches than the treasures in Egypt, become the lawgiver and founder of the Jewish nation; had David done so, going back to his flock, he had never plucked the laurels from the giant's brow, or worn royal crown upon his own; and had Elijah conferred with flesh and blood, then worldly wisdom, cautious prudence, everything but the faith that trusts in God, and laughs at impossibilities, had pronounced his going to Zidon and Zarephath to be an act of downright madness—rushing, not blindfold, but with open eyes on ruin. Surely in vain, says the proverb, the net is spread in the sight of any bird. But from Israel to Zidon, from a land where idolatry was but of recent growth and thousands beside Elijah remained true to their God, to one where all were old, bigoted idolaters, was from bad to worse. If he had run with the footmen and they had wearied him, how was he to contend with horsemen? If they had wearied him in, comparatively speaking, a land of peace, what was he to do in the swellings of Jordan? If his life was in danger in Samaria, how was he to be safe in Zidon? This was a perplexing question. He walked, perhaps, in darkness, and had no light; but he walked boldly on. He stayed himself on God. It was enough that He bade him go there; and there he went as bravely as he strode into Ahab's palace, and bearded that lion in his own den. What a pattern to us, when, though the way be dark, the duty is clear! A most noble example of what a man can dare and a man can do, whose faith is fixed on God!

2. He is sent for sustenance to a widow woman.

Who that has read the story has not admired the tender and touching delicacy of the couriers who, stained with the blood of battle and flushed with victory, communicated to his father the dark tidings of Absalom's death? One messenger has already come; and deeply touched by the anxiety visible in David's countenance, he drops but a hint of evil; announces the victory, but, having no heart to lift the veil and quench at once the hope that breathes in the eager question, Is the young man Absalom safe?

evades it, saying, I saw a great tumult, but I knew not what it was. It falls to Cushi, the second messenger, to deal the blow that reaches the father's heart. But, how delicately done! "Tidings, my lord the king; for the Lord hath avenged thee this day of all them that rose up against thee," are the words with which he bursts, panting, into the king's presence. Not thirsting for vengeance, but thinking only of his misguided son, the father's heart, true as needle to its pole, turns to Absalom. These words, "avenged thee of all them that rose up against thee," have an ominous sound; still he clings to hope, again eagerly inquiring, Is the young man Absalom safe? Cushi's hand is red with blood, yet, though more familiar with inflicting wounds than with healing them, how gently he unveils the dreadful truth! Taking care, by not even pronouncing Absalom's name, or making any allusion to the fact that he was David's son, his first-born, a son of much anxiety and many prayers, to avoid everything that might aggravate the blow and increase the burst of grief which he saw would come, he, as I can fancy, bowing his head and dropping his voice, just says, or, addressing David's God rather than himself, prays, The enemies of my lord the king, and all that rise against thee to do thee hurt, be as that young man is!

What a contrast did this exquisite tenderness on the part of man present to the tone and whole style of God's address to Abraham, when he demanded the sacrifice of his only son! How much in that case did the manner aggravate the matter? With, as we would say, all the skill of oratory, everything is planned to magnify the difficulty of the dreadful task, and, by awaking a father's tenderest emotions, to harrow his feelings and open up the deepest springs of grief. "Take now thy son;" and as if God had a pleasure in wringing the old man's heart, he goes on, "thine only son," reminding Abraham that he is childless when Isaac dies; still more, he names the lad "Isaac," child of promises that nature fears may henceforth lie like withered leaves beneath a father's feet; and still more, as if it needed to be told, or that was a time to tell it, God adds, "whom thou lovest;" and so, by this most tender introduction, prefaces this most dreadful conclusion—"and offer him for a burnt-offering upon one of the mountains which I will tell thee off." Fancy how Abraham started as these words fell like a thunder-peal on his ear, or, rather, struck like a knife through his heart! Had the earth opened at his feet, he could not have been more astonished. And what horror succeeded astonishment! Yet God's purpose was to try, and by trying to strengthen his servant's faith; not to extinguish it, but by this rude wind to blow it up into a brighter flame, that it might shed its light adown the course of time, and make him an example to God's people in all future generations, to be "not faithless, but believing."

And as there, so here every circumstance tends to

increase the difficulty of the prophet's duty. It was not enough that he must seek protection from persecution in a city of idolaters, but, worse and more trying still, he is thrown for bread in famine on a poor widow. Strange! he is not only to expect safety in a land of persecutors, but also plenty in a house of poverty. Our faith, alas! is weak at the strongest. With fightings without and fears within, how ready is it to fail? how often has it failed—overcome by the trials and temptations of life? But when or where was it ever put to a trial like that? A widow woman! "Let thy widows trust in me," "A father of the fatherless, and a judge of the widows, is God in his holy habitation," are words which prove how helpless widows were in those lands where violence so often usurped the place of law. A widow woman! the least likely person in Zarephath to be able to feed this hungry man. The head that had counselled her in difficulties, the arm that had defended her from wrong, the hand that had provided for her wants, laid in the cold grave, mouldering in the dust, in her the prophet seemed to have a forlorn hope indeed. Famine had roused the fiercest passions of our nature: might was right; men fought with men in the streets for bread; and, within-doors, mothers driven mad did worse. If at such a time there were an empty cup and cold hearth in Zarephath, these would be the widow's; one poorer than another, it would be she. Would it have been wonderful had Elijah said, If God is to preserve me, why throw me into the lion's jaws? if he means to support me, why send me to take the bread out of a widow's mouth? why not send me to board with those that have bags of gold and barrels of meal? To cast me for support on a widow, is to lay the burden on a broken back—to bid me turn for help to the hand of the drowning. The ravens are gone, the brook is failed, and I may as well wait death where my unburied bones shall whiten my native soil, as go to seek him in a land of foreigners and a house of famine. What a trial had faith here? and what a triumph? He cast himself on one whom we shall see, gaunt with famine, coming from a house where she has left her dying boy, to gather a few sticks for their last earthly meal; and so doing, Elijah, acting by faith and not by sight, laid the burden on Him who says, Cast thy burden upon the Lord, and he shall sustain thee.

III. Let us learn faith and confidence from the prophet's example—following "them who through faith and patience inherit the promises."

The distant ranges of the Alps or the Andes, on first coming into view, appear but snow-wreaths left by departing winter. The nearer we approach them, they rise higher, and higher, and still higher against the sky, till, resting on stupendous precipices, those snow-crowned summits seem to support the vault of heaven. This effect is often reversed in the case of the believer's trials. Formidable at a distance, dreaded when remote, the nearer his approach to them, not the greater, but the less they grow. The cloudiest day has more gleams, the barest rocks more flowers, the bitterest cup more sweetness, the darkest night more stars, than his fears allowed him to expect; the work is more easily done, the burden more easily borne, than he anticipated; he survives trials that he once thought would have crushed and killed him; and to the last and greatest trial, how applicable often are those words, "Who art thou, O great mountain? before Zerubbabel thou shalt become a plain." He has dreaded death; and death is swallowed up in victory. His latter end is peace. As I have seen the sun as he declined in the west scatter the clouds that hung over the place of his setting, and in his last hour light up heaven and earth in a blaze of glory, so faith, growing stronger as flesh grew weaker, has dissipated all the fears of the dying Christian—leaving his sun to set in a cloudless sky, and weeping friends to exclaim amid their tears, Let me die the death of the righteous, and let my last end be like his!

It happened quite otherwise, however, in the case of the prophet. Bad as it appeared to be cast for maintenance at a time of famine on a widow's help, the trial was worse than his worst fears, perhaps, anticipated — it was like going into a cavern, the further in the darker; into the sea, the further in the deeper. As has befallen others of God's people, the hour of deliverance was preceded by that of greatest trial; just as the pain of an abscess is severest before it bursts, as the darkest hour is before the dawn, and the coldest before sunrise. When the prophet left the banks of Cherith for Zarephath, hope, which often tells a flattering tale, may have suggested that the widow's circumstances might not be so poor as he had at first feared. No doubt famine raged throughout the land, but Zarephath might be an oasis in the desert, supplied with corn through the foresight of a second Joseph; what had occurred before might occur again; and, since the world is preserved for the sake of the saints, as had already happened in Egypt, the fields of the idolater might be made to feed the servants of God. Or this widow might have been left to the comforts of an ample fortune; with gold to buy bread enough even in a famine. Besides, she might have stout, and kind, and gallant sons to sustain her in her widowhood and old age; as I have seen a tree support a wall that had fallen into decay—screening with its leaves, and with its strong, tough arms holding up the stones that had lent it in former days both shelter and support.

Alas! for Elijah, as his weary steps bring him to the gate of Zarephath, if he had no better trust than that. A sight met him there to dash such hopes in the dust, shivering them like a potter's vessel. The widow is at the gate to receive her guest. It is not politeness, or kindness, or, as people meet a great visitor, respect for the man of God that brings her there; no, nor anticipation of the blessing this new burden is to bring. A spectral form, with head bent to the ground, creeps slowly along, ever and anon stretching out from beneath her cloak a skeleton arm to pick up some withered sticks. We have stood in cold and empty room to hear children cry for bread when the mother had none to give them; we have seen hunger looking out from hollow eyes and wasted cheeks, but, never perhaps, such an object as this. The skin like yellow parchment; the bony hand; the eyes sunk in their sockets, whence they emit an unearthly glare; the hollow cheeks; the sepulchral voice; the wasted form, seen sharp through scanty rags; the slow, tottering gait—these bespoke a victim of the famine. And while Elijah gazes on her with mingled emotions of pity and horror, the voice of God is in his ear, saying, Behold the widow woman whom I have commanded to sustain thee!

Was God mocking him when, with finger pointing to this bruised reed, he said, Lean your weight on that? Was it for this he had brought him, buoyed him up with hope, to Zarephath? How did it look as if God were saying to him, as he shall say to his enemies on that day when, having rejected Christ, they find no refuge from impending wrath, I "will laugh at your calamity; I will mock when your fear cometh." What a trial was here! Elijah asks a morsel of bread. Bread? God help her! She has none; her haggard aspect and hollow tones correspond too well with her terrible apology, for him to doubt its truth, "As the Lord thy God liveth, I have not a cake, but an handful of meal in a barrel, and a little oil in a cruse; and, behold, I am gathering two sticks, that I may go in and dress it for me and my son, that we may eat it, and die." How great the faith that staggered not under this blow, but strengthening with the trial, and believing impossibilities, in tones of cheerfulness to which she had been long a stranger, replied, Fear not; go and do as thou hast said; but make me thereof a little cake first, and bring it unto me, and after make for thee and for thy son. For thus saith the Lord God of Israel, The barrel of meal shall not waste, neither shall the cruse of oil fail, until the day that the Lord sendeth rain upon the earth.

And why should not we face our trials and difficulties, whatever they may be, with Elijah's faith? These things were written not for our entertainment, but for our instruction; not so much for our admiration as for our admonition. Let them teach us, saints and sinners both, to place unbounded trust in every passage and promise of God's word that suits our circumstances—to venture our souls upon them. No doubt Elijah, having much in God's past dealings to sustain his faith, could say with David, I will remember the years of the right hand of the most High. He who made the wild ravens serve him could make poverty sustain him. The man who had seen these shy birds sweeping past their nests and clamorous young to lay their plunder at his feet, and wait at his table as dutiful and familiar servants, might look on this gaunt and ghastly widow to trust her for bread—leaning his whole weight on a support frail as the thread of a spider's web. But have we not grounds of trust in God as good and strong as he had? He has given his Son for us—his own beloved Son to die for us. The eye that saw the ravens desert their brood to cater for a hungry prophet, saw no proof of kindness and power and love to compare with Calvary's bloody cross. Miracles we do not look for: but that God, if you will truly and earnestly seek him, will forgive your sins for Jesus' sake; that whosoever believeth in his Son shall never perish; that he will cast out none that come to him; that he will save you now, and just as you are; that he will shut the door in no man's face; that he will make his grace sufficient for you, and perfect his strength in your weakness; that with or without miracles he will make good every promise in his word —these are truths I cannot doubt. All blessings which the Father has promised, and the Son has purchased, the Spirit is ready to bestow. He who spared not his own Son, shall he not with him freely give you all things? Now then, "Arise, be up and doing;" and whether your sins call you to the fountain of blood, or your sorrows to the fountain of consolation, or your weakness to the fountain of strength, "arise," as I can fancy Elijah rose, and, leaving Cherith's dry bed

L

behind, took his way to Zarephath; and as he went beguiled the road and woke the echoes of the lonely valleys with such songs as these—

"The lions young may hungry be,
  And they may lack their food;
But they that truly seek the Lord
  Shall not lack any good.

"Oh! taste and see that God is good;
  Who trusts in him is bless'd.
Fear God his saints; none that him fear
  Shall be with want oppress'd."

X.

THE TRUE TEST.

"The tree is known by its fruit."—MATT. xii. 33.

THERE are various kinds of knowledge; nor, notwithstanding the adage, "A little knowledge is a dangerous thing," is there any kind or measure of it without its value. I would sit at the feet of the humblest man to learn what he knew and I did not. The most important thing, however, to know, is one's self, although, I may remark, no man can know his own character aright, without first making himself acquainted with that of God. It is in his light that we see light clearly. Hence it was not till Job had obtained full and clear views of the holiness, purity, and providence of God, that he formed a just estimate of himself—exclaiming, I had heard of thee with the hearing of the ear, but now mine eye seeth thee: wherefore I abhor myself, and repent in dust and ashes.

To an ingenuous youth who sought his advice as to the course of study he should pursue, and what knowledge he should seek first to obtain, an old Greek sage replied, Know thyself! No Christian could have given a better answer. What a miserable thing it is for a man to know how to make money, and make it too—to know science so well that he is familiar with the secrets of nature, can measure the distance of a star, and follow a wandering comet on its fiery track—to know statesmanship so well that his country, in a crisis of her affairs, might call him to the helm, as before all others the pilot that could weather the storm,—and yet not to know whether he is at peace with God; whether, should he die to-night, he is saved or lost; is going to heaven or to hell! I undervalue no knowledge; but were I lying in jail under sentence of death, and, having got no answer to my application for mercy, did not know whether I was to be spared or to be hanged to-morrow, what would I care about the discovery of a new planet or new metal, a change of ministry, the rise or fall of prices, the rise or fall of kingdoms? The one question which would interest me, now awakening my hopes and now my gloomiest apprehensions, would be this: Am I saved? or, What shall I do to be saved? But we all lie under sentence of condemnation—death has passed on all men, because all have sinned. And so, though through a Christian profession we have a name to live, yet we may in fact be dead—dead in the eye of the law; and in such circumstances, I say with the Greek, that, to know ourselves, to know what we are and where we are, is of all knowledge the most important. If there shall be no more salvation out of Christ on a day of judgment than there was found out of the ark on that day when the avenging waters pursued the shrieking crowd to the tops of the highest hills, and washed off the last living man from the last dry spot of land, how important for us to know whether we are in Christ—united to him, not in name and by profession only, but by faith, in deed, and in truth! To try this, we have a plain and infallible test in these words of our Lord, The tree is known by its fruit. On this subject I remark—

I. It is possible to ascertain our real state and character.

In the Southern Hemisphere, where the plants and animals present some remarkable resemblances to those which lived and died and were entombed in the rocks before man's appearance on the earth, a strange creature lives, that seems half bird, half quadruped; and, rooted to the rocks of our own shores, in the briny pools that are left by each receding tide, we find objects, in point of colour and form, beautiful as any of the ornaments of our gardens—of such a character, that many would be puzzled to settle whether they are most nearly, as flowers of the deep, allied to the sea-weeds which wave over them, or to those animals which, in every shape and size, from shrimps to whales, have their home in the ocean. In the fields of nature are birds that always walk and never fly, and quadrupeds that always fly and never walk; plants that, sensitive like animals, shrink from the touch, and animals that, fixed like a tree to the rock, live, die, and decay on the spot of their birth; flowers that might be readily mistaken for butterflies, with painted, fluttering wings, just alighted on the plant, and insects which it is impossible at first sight to distinguish, some from green, and others from withered leaves. He who, though a God, not of confusion, but of order, delights in variety, has so linked together the vegetable and animal kingdoms, and also their various departments, that many objects might be placed in the hands of a peasant, nor could he tell whether they were plants or animals, or to what section of these two great kingdoms they belonged. There is no such difficulty when we attempt to settle the question whether we belong to the one or the other of those two grand classes into which all mankind, kings and beggars, men and women, white skins and dark skins, may be divided. A broad line, like the gulf that separates heaven from hell, divides saints and sinners. Addressing the latter, a saint of God may say, as Abraham did to the rich man in torment, "Between us and you there is a great gulf fixed, so that they which would pass from hence to you cannot;" yet, thank God, he can add, Unlike yon gulf which no bridge of mercy spans, you can pass to us that would come from thence.

Unless Scripture is a mockery and its figures have no meaning whatever, it is not impossible, nor should it even be difficult, to determine our spiritual state, now and at once. Who has any difficulty in settling whether it is day or night: whether he enjoys sound health or pines on a bed of sickness: whether he is a free man or a slave? No man could mistake a Briton, sitting under the tree of liberty which was planted by the hands of our fathers and watered with their blood, for the negro who stands up weeping in the auction mart, to be sold with his master's cattle, or crouches in the rice swamp, bleeding under his master's lash. Degraded by a system that curses both man and master, the black man may be content to eat the bread and wear the brand of bondage. Still he, as much as we do, knows the difference between fetters and freedom; he feels that he is a slave, and I feel that I am free: even so may we know whether we belong to the class of saints or to that of sinners—for sin is darkness, sickness, bondage. What plainer evidence of this could be desired than these words, "The tree is known by his fruit." That is a fact with which we are all familiar. To stock the garden with fruit-trees, I repair to the nursery, but not in spring when all are robed alike in green; nor in summer when the bad equally with the best are covered with a flush of blossoms: it is when the corn turns yellow, and sheaves stand in the stubble fields, and fair blossoms are gone, and withered leaves sail through the air and strew the ground—it is in autumn I go to select the trees, judging them by their fruit. And as certainly—may I not say as easily?—as the tree is known by his fruit, may we know our spiritual state and character, if we will only be honest, nor act like the merchant who, suspecting his affairs to be verging on bankruptcy, shuts his eyes to the danger; takes no stock, and strikes no balance.

How otherwise could any man lay his head in peace on his pillow: go to sleep when he did not know but that the next time he opened his eyes it should be in hell? This would be a dreadful state in which to pass our life. In such circumstances, where were the pleasures of piety, the peace of God that passeth understanding, the triumphs of a Christian's dying hours? If death be, as some say, and as it must be if it is impossible to know our state, "a leap in the dark," what madness his who stands on the brink of another world, not shrinking, trembling, hesitating, but singing, O death, where is thy sting? O grave, where is thy victory? I do not aver that all God's people enjoy a full assurance of salvation. Still, unless a man can, by the witness of God's Spirit with his own, attain to some good hope that he has passed through grace from death to life, that the sentence of condemnation has been annulled, that his sins have been forgiven, that he has been reconciled to God through the blood of Jesus Christ, that a crown and mansion are waiting for him above the skies, how, in the name of reason, could he rejoice and be exceeding glad? The thing is impossible. He could not; any more than the seaman can when his ship is driving on a lee shore and he has dropped his last anchor, until, brought up, she swings round on the very edge of foaming breakers, rides on the top of the billows, and with her bow to the storm. His anchor holds, and he knows that he is safe: and, blessed be God, we also have hope as an anchor of the soul both sure and steadfast, which entereth into that which is within the veil.

II. Our religious profession is not always a test of our state.

1. It may be a test in certain circumstances.

Look, for example, at two men on parade! They wear the same dress and arms: and both, the result of drill and discipline, have acquired such a martial air that you cannot tell which is the hero and which the coward. But change the scene! Leave the parade ground for the field of battle! and when, as bugles sound the charge, I see, through clouds of smoke and amid the clash of arms, the sword of one flashing, and his plume dancing in the very front of the fight, while his comrade, pale and paralysed with fear, is only borne forward in the tumult like a sea-weed on the rushing billow,—how easy now to tell beneath whose martial dress there beats a soldier's heart? Or take, for another example, two houses that stand on the banks of the same stream. Under a cloudless sky, amid the calm of the glen in a summer day, with no sound falling on the ear but the bleatings of the flock, the baying of a sheep-dog, the muffled sound of a distant waterfall, the gentle murmur of the shallow waters over their pebbly bed, each house in its smiling garden offers, to one weary of the din and dust of cities, an equally pleasant and, to appearance, an equally secure retreat. But let the weather change: and after brewing for hours, from out the darkness that has deepened into an ominous and frightful gloom, let the storm burst! Suddenly, followed by a crash like that of falling skies, a stream of lightning, dazzling the eye, glares out: and now the war of elements begins. Peal rolls on peal: flash follows flash: and to the roar of incessant thunders is added the rush of a deluge, and the hoarse voices of a hundred streams that leap foaming from hill and rock down into the bed of the river. Red, rolling, swelling, it bursts its dykes, overflows all its banks, and, attacking the foundations of both houses, breaches the walls of one, and at length tumbles the whole fabric, all of a heap, into the roaring flood: and while the houseless family that had fled from its rocking walls gather, shivering, on a neighbouring height to see where once stood their pleasant home only the rush and hear only the roar of waters,—how easy, as we look on the other, erect, and defiant in this wide-spread sea, to know that the one had been built on sand, but the other founded on a rock.

So, though the profession does not prove the possession of religion in a time of peace, shew me a man, like the house standing its ground against the sweep of floods, or the soldier following his colours into the thick of battle, who holds fast the profession of his faith in the face of obloquy, of persecution, of death itself, and there is little room to doubt that his piety is genuine—that he has the root of the matter in him. I care nothing for Hosannas when accompanied by crowds who cast their clothes on the dusty road and rend the air with acclamations—Jesus, enjoying a gleam of popularity, seems marching to a crown—the tongues that cry, Hosanna! to-day, changing their note, may cry, Crucify him! to-morrow. But who, not turning with the turning tide, like the blessed women that lamented and bewailed him, follows our Lord to the cross, goes without the camp bearing his reproach, is tested in a fire which only gold can stand. What are these which are arrayed in white robes? and whence came they? These are they, is the reply, which came out of great tribulation, and have washed their robes, and made them white in the blood of the Lamb. Therefore are they before the throne of God, and serve him night and day in the temple: and he that sitteth on the throne shall dwell among them. They shall hunger no more, neither thirst any more: neither shall the sun light on them, nor any heat. For the Lamb which is in the midst of the throne shall feed them, and shall lead them unto living fountains of waters: and God shall wipe away all tears from their eyes.

2. The profession of religion is not a test of the reality of religion in our times.

I should be sorry to believe that no man could be a lover of Jesus Christ who did not go to the table of communion to commemorate his death. Some go there who should not: and some, restrained from the enjoyment of that blessed ordinance by unsound views of its nature, or of their own qualifications, do not go who should. I would be sorry also to believe that a man cannot be a true, unless he is also a bold Christian, and makes a fearless profession of piety. Elijah did indeed buckle on his armour and stand forth alone —openly confronting the vengeance of the crown and hatred of the people. Yet, concealed from the public eye, and unknown even to this brave defender of the faith, God had seven thousand men in Israel with knees that had never bowed to Baal, and mouths that had never kissed him. In later times Nicodemus sought an interview with our Lord under the cloud of night, and Joseph of Arimathea was a believer some time before he openly avowed it. Like flowers which close their leaves whenever it rains, or birds that seek shelter and their nests when storms rise, there are Christians so timid by natural constitution, that they shrink from scorn, and could as soon face a battery of cannon as the jeers and laughter of the ungodly.

Granting this, still it is true, that where there is no profession of serious religion, we have little reason to expect its reality. We may say of it what Solomon said of the contentious woman who proclaims her presence in house or hamlet by her loud, sharp tongue, Whosoever hideth her hideth the wind, and hideth the ointment of his right hand, which bewrayeth itself. Out of the abundance of the heart, as our Lord says, the mouth speaketh. What is in will be out; there being always some seam through which the water will leak, some chink through which the light will shine. A look, a word, will disclose the secret; and sometimes a devout man by his silence more even than by his words will proclaim himself. So that, as no man could enter a company with ointment in his hand, but, however close he held his fist, the fragrance would oose through his fingers, a true, hearty, genuine piety will reveal itself notwithstanding that an attempt may be made to conceal it, and that the humble saint has none of that courage which won for Knox, from the lips of an enemy, this brave eulogium, There lies one who never feared the face of man.

But if a man can have no piety who makes no profession of it, it is still more plain that the scoffers have none, who ridicule zealous Christians, as hypocrites or fanatics, Pharisees or fools. Such profane scoffers have no more love to Christ than had the iron-hearted and iron-handed men who pressed the thorns into his bleeding brow, and casting over his mangled form an old purple robe, made a mock of the Lord of glory. Whether it has been a cup of water, held to the dying lips of a poor saint, or a sneer flung at a disciple's head, Jesus shall say, Inasmuch as ye have done it unto one of the least of these, my brethren, ye have done it unto me.

Perhaps there never was a time when the mere profession of religion was a less satisfactory test of its reality than at present. There have been dark and evil days, and these not long gone, when religion was, if I may so express myself, at a discount: piety was not fashionable: profane swearing and deep drinking were the accomplishments of a gentleman; the man who assembled his household for prayer was accounted a hypocrite, the woman who did so a fool: missionary societies were repudiated by the courts of the Church, and eyed with suspicion by the officers of the Crown; Robert Haldane was denied an opportunity of consecrating his fortune to the cause of Christ in India; Carey and Marshman, while seeking to convert the Hindoos, were driven from the British territories, and had to seek protection from a foreign Power; and such as formed missionary associations launched them on society with the anxieties and prayers of her who, cradling her infant in an ark of bulrushes, committed him to the waters of the Nile and the providence of her God. Power, rank, fashion, science, literature, and mammon were all arrayed in arms against everything that appeared in the form, and breathed the spirit of a devoted piety.

Thank God, it is not so now! He has touched the

The True Test.   175

heart of the Egyptian, and she has adopted the outcast as her son. From holes and caves of the earth, religion has found her way into palaces and the mansions of the great and noble. Science has become a priestess at her altar. Literature has courted her alliance. Infidelity assumes even a Christian-like disguise. Iniquity, as ashamed, is made to hide her face. The tide has turned ; and those who now make a profession of zealous and active piety, find themselves no longer opposed to the stream and spirit of the age. This is a subject of gratitude. Yet it suggests caution in judging of ourselves ; and warns us to take care, since a profession of religion is rather fashionable than otherwise, that in making it we are not the creatures of fashion, but new creatures in Jesus Christ. When the crown sat on the head of Mordecai, and he himself sat on the royal steed, and Haman walked at his bridle rein as he rode the streets of Shushan in royal state—heralds proclaiming, " Thus it shall be done to the man whom the king delighteth to honour," the Jew knew right well to what he owed the reverence paid him by many a supple Persian. And when religion rides through the land in triumph, many will bend the knee, shew her respect, and do her reverence, who would pass her in haughty scorn were she sitting at the porter's gate. Hence the necessity for trying ourselves by such a test as my text suggests. The tree is known, not by its leaves, nor we by our professions ; not by its blossoms, nor we by the promises of which they are lovely images; but by its fruit, and we by those things which the fruit represents—our hearts and habits, our true life and character. The tree is known by his fruit: moreover every tree that bringeth not forth good fruit is hewn down and cast into the fire.

III. The true evidence of our state is to be found in our heart and habits. The tree is known by his fruit,—by their fruits ye shall know them.

We have often sat in judgment on others. It is of more consequence that we form a right estimate of ourselves—leaving others to God; for in the words of an apostle, Who art thou that judgeth another man's servant? to his own master he standeth or falleth. In attempting to form a correct estimate of our own state and character, in the words of the Greek sage, to know ourselves, let us bring to this solemn task all the care and the conscientiousness with which a jury weigh the evidence in a case of life and death. They return from their room to the court to give in a verdict, amid breathless silence, which sends him whom they left pale and trembling at the bar to liberty, or to the gallows; yet, sacred as human life is, on our judgment here hangs a more momentous issue. A mistake there may send a man to the scaffold, but one here to perdition,—that involves the life of the body, this of the immortal soul. Judges sometimes find it difficult to know how to shape their charge, and juries how to shape their verdicts—the evidence is conflicting—not clear either way. The case is obscure, perplexing; perhaps a bloody mystery, from which no hand but God's can raise the veil. But light and darkness, life and death, are not more unlike than the heart and habits of believers, on the one hand, and those of unbelievers, on the other; and with such a catalogue of the works of the flesh and the fruits of the Spirit as Paul has given us, how can it be difficult for a man to settle under which of these two classes his are to be ranked—with which they most closely correspond? The works of the flesh, says the apostle, are manifest, Adultery, fornication, uncleanness, lasciviousness, idolatry, witchcraft, hatred, variance, emulations, wrath, strife, seditions, heresies, envyings: murders, drunkenness, revellings, and such like. But the fruit of the Spirit is love, joy, peace: long-suffering, gentleness: goodness, faith, meekness, temperance. A man may fancy himself possessed of talents which he has not, and a woman of beauty which she has not. But with all our strong bias to form a favourable and flattering opinion of ourselves, each "to think more highly of himself than he ought to think," it seems as impossible for a man who is an adulterer, a fornicator, unclean, a drunkard, whose bosom burns with unholy and hateful passions, to imagine himself virtuous, as to mistake night for day, a bloated, fetid corpse, for one in the bloom and rosy beauty of her youth. In regard to these tests, let me also remark, we are to look for a correspondence between them and our hearts and habits: for no more. Few have plunged into such excess of wickedness as to have their lives characterised by all these works of the flesh; for there is a moderation in vice as well as in virtue; and some vices, as one class of weeds eradicates another, unfit a man for indulging in other vices. Nor, on the other hand, are you to expect to find in any one all these fruits of the Spirit in luxuriant and equal abundance; still as he who is but a child in sin is still a child of the devil, he is a son of God who is but a babe in grace.

It is only often by a careful application of delicate tests that the chemist discovers a deadly poison or a precious metal; but how easy is it by a few simple questions to bring out our real character! Have you suffered a heavy wrong, for example, at the hands of another? You remember it. But where? Is it at the throne of grace; and to pray with him whose blood fell alike on the head of foe and friend, Father forgive them, they know not what they do? Again, are you asked to contribute money to the cause of Christ? while some calculate how little they can give to satisfy their conscience and meet the expectations of society, do you calculate how much you can spare for that blessed Saviour who did not spare himself for you? Again, when tempted to sin, while some wish there were no hell to deter them from the unbridled enjoyment of its pleasures, do you rather long for that pure, blessed heaven, where there entereth nothing to hurt or to defile? Again, when you see transgressors, is it with indifference, or with somewhat of the feelings of him who said, I saw transgressors and was grieved—rivers of waters ran down mine eyes, because they keep not thy law, O Lord? Again, when you think of perishing souls, is yours the spirit of Cain, or of Christ? can you no more stand by with folded hands to see sinners perishing than men drowning? are you moved by such generous impulse as draws the hurrying crowd to the pool where one is sinking, and moves some brave man, at the jeopardy of life, to leap in and pluck him from the jaws of death? There is no better evidence that we have received the nature as well as the name of Christ, than an anxious wish to save lost souls, and a sympathy with the joy of angels over every sinner that is converted. Let me illustrate this by two examples — pictures drawn from life.

Years ago, and in a parish which I knew, there lived a woman notorious in the neighbourhood for profane swearing, habits of drunkenness, and manners rude; coarse as well as irreligious. She feared not God, neither regarded man; and trained up her children for the devil. One evening she happened to be within ear-shot of a preacher; and as he was emptying his quiver among the crowd, an arrow from the bow drawn at a venture was lodged in her heart. Remarkable example of free, sovereign, subduing grace! she was converted. Her case, as much as that of the thief on the cross, of the jailor at Philippi, of Saul on his way to Damascus, was one of instant conversion—day burst on her soul without a dawn. She hastened home. She found her family asleep, and saw in each child a never-dying soul, that her own hand had rocked into deeper, fatal slumbers. Seized with an intense desire to have them saved, she could not delay the matter till to-morrow; and so, rushing on the sleepers as if the bed beneath them had been in flames, she shook them, woke them, crying, Arise, call upon thy God! And there at the midnight hour, with her children kneeling round her, her eyes streaming with tears, her voice trembling with emotion, did that poor mother cry to God, that he would have mercy also on them, and pluck these brands from the burning.

Near by the dwelling where a mother roused her children from their beds to flee, not from a house on fire, but from the fire that is never quenched, stood the cottage of one whose joy over a converted sinner carried us away to the heavens, where angels rejoice over one sinner that repenteth. He had long been a Christian; not so his wife, from whose side he had often stolen in the dead of night to pray for her salvation. He continued instant in prayer. Mothers, sisters, all who carry others in their prayers to the throne of grace, Pray on! God's time to answer—the time to favour her at length came. She was smitten; seized with

The True Test.

anxiety; pierced with convictions; but she could find no peace. She walked in darkness and had no light; and giving herself up for lost, once said, for instance, when her husband and she had lain down for sleep, If you should die before to-morrow, it will be happy for you; if I should, farewell, an everlasting farewell—I shall open my eyes in torment! But the time of her redemption drew nigh. She had sown in tears, and was to reap in joy. A minister hearing of her distress, went to visit her. She was in the garden. Her husband left the house to call her. Who seeks me? she asked. Without forethought, as if the words had fallen from heaven on his lips, he replied, Jesus Christ seeks you! She started: an ashy paleness overspread her face: and, deeply affected, she followed him in silence to the house. There the man of God held up before her a bleeding, dying, loving, Saviour. Prayer followed, and praise followed prayer; for while they entreated God with strong crying and tears, the grave opened, and she that was dead came forth—to say, I confess that Jesus is the Lord, and to sing with Mary, My soul doth magnify the Lord; and my spirit hath rejoiced in God my Saviour; for he hath regarded the low estate of his handmaiden—he that is mighty hath done to me great things, and holy is his name. And what did you do? I asked the husband. Do, sir? he replied; I sprang to my feet; I clasped her in my arms; I exclaimed, This is our marriage day; and unable to restrain my joy, I cried

Hosanna to the Son of David! Praise him, all ye his angels; praise him, sun, moon, and stars; praise him, all ye orbs of light!

By their fruits ye shall know them. Grapes do not grow on thorns, nor figs on thistles—nor such fruits in any but renewed hearts. So to feel proves what no profession can, that the same mind is in us that was in Jesus Christ: nor is there room to doubt that if you bear such saintly and heavenly fruit, you are one with him who, communicating the influences of the Spirit to his people, as the tree does its sap to the boughs, hath said, I am the Vine; ye are the branches. Abide in me, and I in you.

XI.

SPIRITUAL VISION.

"Open thou mine eyes, that I may behold wondrous things out of thy law."—PSALM cxix. 18.

THERE is a baronial castle in our country lost in the bosom of a hoary wood, that stands, in its lonely desertion, a picture of the family whose arms are still seen on its mouldering walls, and whose fortunes have fallen into a like decay. Many a wild legend is told about this old pile by the country people around their hearths on the long nights of winter. They say that strange sounds, now cries of violence, and now peals of laughter, are still heard in these dismantled halls, and that belated travellers have seen a female form, in antique attire, walking in the moonlight on the mossy lawn, or gazing out of these empty windows—one whose crimes deny her poor bones the rest of the grave.

Among other strange things, they tell an incident which is not only credible, but true. It befell one generation of the family that, to the inexpressible disappointment and grief of his parents, the eldest child, their son and heir, was born deaf; sadder still, so was the next; the third, also—one deaf mute succeeding another, till the cradle, where no lullaby was sung, and the nursery, where no merry laughter mingled with the pattering of little feet, were like the hand of an avenging Providence. The story goes that, after this, at the birth of each succeeding child, the father, devoured by anxiety, and impatient to know the best or worst, was wont to enter the natal chamber, and, while he turned a look of dread on his infant, to discharge fire-arms close by its ear. He sought to know, by its stillness or sudden start, whether the curse still hung over his house. Unhappy man! Yet still more unhappy father, all whose children are born blind! Unless to see them all lying around in their shrouds, a more touching sight you cannot fancy than a whole family stone-blind, from the eldest to the infant that sits prattling on a mother's knee—as unconscious of its misfortune as one that, brought to receive a mother's last embrace, smiles in her face, or one that laughs as she presses it to her bosom when their ship, taking the last lurch, is going down into the deep. Keenly alive as we are to the evils of a bodily infirmity, and ready, like the woman in the Gospel, who spent all that she had to be healed, to pay any money to cure a child's blindness, or to suffer any operation to remove our own—such a sight would sadden us. And it is sad to think, leaving the regions of fancy for facts, that there are a million of our fellow-creatures blind, many of whom never saw the sun, nor saw a father's face, nor were ever cheered by a mother's smile. Yet, were we as sensible to spiritual as to natural evils, we should feel that a far greater calamity lies on us, and on our children. It may give us no trouble. Blind ourselves, we may be as insensible to their wants as to our own. Still, there is no parent who may not say of his child what they said to whose son our Saviour had imparted sight—" We know that he was born blind." Blindness to the things of the spiritual world lies by nature on us all. Having eyes, we see not, and ears, we hear not; therefore, unless we would miss the way to heaven, and go stumbling over into hell, what need have we to go to Jesus with this prayer, Open thou mine eyes, that I may behold wondrous things out of thy law.

I. We are all born spiritually blind.

When Samson, too confident in himself, ventured on temptation, he fell into the snare of the Philistines. As if ignorant, that, to use the words of Solomon, " A whore is a deep ditch, and a strange woman is a narrow pit," he trusted his paramour; and disclosing the secret of his mighty strength, was shorn of his locks. She sold him; and he had nothing else to expect at such hands. The loss of vigour follows loss of virtue; and he, like others from whom the Lord has departed, became an easy prey to his enemies. With no pity for fallen greatness, they triumphed over their once dreaded foe, heaping insults on his head. But his locks might grow again, and strength return to the broad shoulders over which they fell like a lion's mane? In that case he may escape; and once free, burning with rage and breathing vengeance, woe to Delilah, to her house and people! They took effectual means to prevent this. They put out his eyes—with these quenching their own fears and their prisoner's hopes. And see the strong man now! poor, blind, helpless; once the terror of men, and now the laughing-stock of women; as a drudge, a slave, sunk to the meanest condition; bound in fetters, he grinds his masters' corn—his associates the lowest felons, his home a common prison, and his lot made more bitter by self-reproach, by remorse, by the memory of former greatness, of happiness and honour exchanged for exile and captivity. .

What a picture of misery! and further, what a picture of man! a mirror where unconverted men, had they eyes to see, might behold, not Samson, but themselves in Samson. Was he taken captive of the Philistines?—so are they of their vices. Did he pass his days in the service of his enemies?—slaves of Satan, they serve one who, in the words of David, hates them with cruel hatred. Was he bound in fetters of brass?—what are fetters of brass or iron to the chains of the drunkard, of the licentious, of the miser, of the lover of this world? Was he blinded as well as bound?—so are they. "Eyes have they, but they see not;" "the god of this world," as St Paul says, "hath blinded the minds of them which believe not;" they are insensible to their state. But here fails the parallel. Samson felt his degradation keenly; longed for liberty; poured many a tear from those sightless eyes; strained at his chain; groped about to find a door of escape; cursed his folly; hated the thought of Delilah, and would, I believe, have struck her down had she come within his reach. How different the poor sinner! He hugs his chain, and delights in the vices that enslave him; to Christ's cry, Behold, I have set before thee an open door, he does not leap up, but turns away his ear; and, as if he had lost his sense as well as his sight, in prison, in captivity, in misery, awaiting a dreadful doom, he says, "I am rich, and increased with goods, and have need of nothing," at the very time God is saying, "Thou art wretched, and miserable, and poor, and blind, and naked."

When man lost his innocence, he lost also his sight. Blindness is the effect of sin. Hence the appropriateness of the figure, so common in Scripture, which compares sin to leprosy—that foulest and deadliest of diseases. At its first appearance but a small spot on the brow, it spreads betimes over all the body; covering its victim with a universal sore, and eating its way at length into the very seat of life. Isaiah's picture of a man or nation sunk in sin was no fancy sketch. A leper stood for this portrait; "the whole head is sick, and the whole heart faint. From the sole of the foot even unto the head there is no soundness in it; but wounds, and bruises, and putrefying sores." As this hideous malady extends its ravages, the fingers and toes and limbs rot off, till little else remains but a mutilated trunk; within which, the eyes also eaten out, the miserable victim drags on a wretched existence in total, hopeless blindness. Even so sin affects the whole man, and destroys the image of God, as a cancer does the beauty of the sweetest face and finest form—making us as loathsome as once we were lovely in the sight of God and holy angels. Proud man may revolt from the portrait; but that does not prove it to be exaggerated. It is not untrue, because it is abhorrent. Abhorrent? who ever got their eyes opened to see themselves but they abhorred themselves—saying, with one who was no profligate or prodigal, but the best and most upright of men, even Job himself: "I have heard of thee by the hearing of the ear; but now mine eye seeth thee: wherefore I abhor myself, and repent in dust and ashes."

II. Leaving now the cause, let us consider some of the characteristics of this blindness.

Blindness deprives its subjects of many pleasures which God's goodness lavishes on us, and, through our eyes, pours into our hearts. To them the sun has no brightness; the meadow no gay flowers; the great vault of heaven no stars; and, worst of all, the faces that are beaming love on them are blank, without expression. In heaven the saints have no night, but

Spiritual Vision. 189

on earth the blind have no day; only darkness; night unchanging, endless night.

Blindness makes the condition of its subjects one of painful dependence. Without his eyes, Samson was more helpless than the child who, holding his big hand, led him forward to make sport in the crowded theatre. We cannot but pity the helpless blind; yet how often is our pity misplaced? Touched by his sorrows, the women of Jerusalem wept for Jesus; yet had more cause to weep for themselves. Our blood boiling with indignation at the story of his cruel wrongs, we demand freedom for the slave; and yet may be greater slaves ourselves than one whose limbs are manacled, but whose soul is free. And on some who regard them with gentle pity, the blind, enjoying heaven's light within, might turn their sightless balls to say with Jesus, Weep not for me, but weep for yourselves. Oh, what blindness so deep, so dark, so incurable, so miserable, so fatal, as that of sin? as yours, unless you have been brought from death to life—out of darkness into marvellous light? And yet so general is spiritual blindness, that "darkness covereth the earth, and gross darkness the people."

Blindness exposes its subjects to deception. Look into that tent where, with head silvered and eyes dimmed through age, an old man sits, as with trembling hands he bestows the blessing on a son who eyes him with cunning look, and to his suspicious touch offers neck and arms masked with a borrowed skin.

The voice is Jacob's, but the hands are Esau's; and so, lulling Isaac's suspicions, and passing for the elder brother, the younger takes cruel advantage of the old man's blindness, to steal a brother's birthright and a father's blessing. A case of theft, the basest, and most cruel, that crime dogged the good man's heels through life, onward to his grave! Yet, in its direful consequences this foul trick is not to be mentioned with the deceptions which the devil practises on men. Taking advantage of their blindness, their cruel enemy passes himself off as a friend—forsooth the friend of sinners. Believe the smiling fiend, and he would not hurt you, but rather minister to your happiness; you shall not surely die; life has time to sin now and repent afterwards; nor is God the just, righteous, and exacting judge your fears and your ministers represent. And thus Satan makes thousands believe that all is right, that the path they tread is one of safety, when all the while, step by step, down, but gently down, he conducts his blind, deluded, singing, dancing, joyous victims on to the brink of ruin, and to that last, fatal step which plunges them into hell.

Again, blindness exposes us to danger. Provided the monster does not growl, a blind man will walk right into a lion's den. Though scared by the flood whose hoarse and angry roar warns him back, he will step into a dark and silent pool. He will linger on the sands around which the tide is stealing, till the waters wash his feet; and, all retreat cut off by deep

Spiritual Vision.

lagoons, he has no answer to the friendly voices of the shore but the words of one who died in despair, Too late, too late! Shew a child a flower of brightest hues, heedless as childhood is, he plucks it not, but starts back in horror—his eyes have met those of a serpent, gleaming from out its painted leaves. But, tempted by its fragrance, the blind man stoops to pluck, and stung, he dies—he scented the odour, but saw not the serpent. A blind man will starve with bread within his reach; parched and perishing with thirst, he will pass the well that invites his lips to drink; drowning, with a rope thrown within his grasp, and the cries of eager voices in his ear, Lay hold of life! he will sink into a watery grave—lost, when he might have been saved. Such is the case of the unconverted! Who so blind as sinners? May God open their eyes! Oh, if they saw the hatefulness of sin and the beauty of Jesus, the danger of their souls and their great need of salvation, if they were other than blind, stone-blind, how would they pause in their career; and like one who, the mist suddenly opening to reveal his true position, starts with horror to see his feet on the dreadful brink, the very edge of a precipice, how would sinners, with eyes open to the greatness of their jeopardy, turn at the cry God is now sounding in all our ears, Turn ye, turn ye from your evil ways; for why will ye die, O house of Israel!

III. The eyes of the blind being opened, they behold wondrous things out of the law of God.

There was an eminent philosopher who had devoted a lifetime to the pursuits of science, and not, as he thought, in vain. She had crowned his brow with laurels, and inscribed his name in the temple of fame. In the evening of his days, at the eleventh hour, God was pleased to call him, open his eyes, convert him; and now, he who was deeply read in science and conversant with its loftiest speculations, as he bent his gray head over the Bible, (the law spoken of in the text,) declared that, if he had his life to live over again, he would spend it in the study of the Word of God. He felt like a miner, who, after toiling long and to little purpose in search of gold, with one stroke of his pick-axe lays open a vein of the precious metal and becomes rich at once—the owner of a vein that grows the richer the deeper the mine is driven. Such a treasure the Bible offers to those whose eyes God has opened to its wonders of grace and glory. It is inexhaustible. The further, leaving the shore with its sounding beach and shallow waters, you go out to sea, the deeper it grows; the higher you climb a hill, the wider grows the prospect of rolling land, and liquid plain; the deeper, at least in some instances, the shaft is sunk into the bowels of the earth, richer minerals reward your labour. Even so, the further and the longer we pursue our investigations into divine truth, and study the Bible, the more it grows in interest and in value. The devout Christian discovers new beauties every day. We never tire of its pages; at every new reading we make new discoveries, and its truths are always as fresh as new-blown roses which nobody ever tires smelling, as each morning brings them out blushing red and bathed in dew. Only let a man's eyes be opened, and such wondrous things will be seen in the Bible that he would part with all his books rather than with that, esteeming it better not only than any, but than all of them, and deeming those his best hours of study which were spent in exploring the mysteries and mercies of redeeming love.

Some may regard this as little better than raving. With Bibles, to use Whitfield's words, on whose dust you might write damnation, put aside for the newspaper or the novel, they have no sympathy with this. How can they have? In the words of the prophet, They seeing, see not; and hearing, they hear not; neither do they understand. The ancients tell of one who played such exquisite music, that his skill drew the birds from the sky, even serpents from their holes; and gathered round him in strange companionship and silent wonder the wild beasts of the field and forest. Suppose this were no fable, and that, lyre in hand, Orpheus were to walk our streets; stopping the rushing tide of men and business, as the waters were stayed in Jordan's bed. These notes fall on the ears of the deaf as on those of the dead; the mute passes by, let the charmer charm never so wisely—his only wonder what arrests the gaping crowd, or what they see to admire in these fingers that run up and down the strings. He thinks, as people with no musical ear are inclined to do, on seeing an assembly thrown into raptures by some grand melody, that, as Felix said of Paul, and the world is apt to say of sincere and ardent Christians, they are mad—beside themselves.

Now, as the deaf have no sympathy with those that hear, the blind have none with those that see. On the wall of a church, for example, in a foreign town, there hangs a wonderful painting of Christ's last hours on the cross; with a countenance full of love, of the deepest awe, and greatest sorrow, John is gazing on the spectacle, while our Lord's mother, supported by Mary Magdalene, lies fainting at his feet. On the curtain being rolled up that covers it, you cannot speak; you cannot take off your eyes; you forget the painter in the painting; and some such emotions of awe, pity, and wonder take possession of you as seized on the centurion, who feeling the earth quake, and hearing the cry of Calvary, declared as he left the scene, Truly this was the Son of God. Yet take one of the blind mendicants who, cap in hand, beg by that old cathedral door, and set him before the picture; unveil its wonders before his sightless eyeballs; and he stands as unmoved as the cold, hard, stony pillar on which the canvas hangs. Or, from the works of man, take the blind out to those of God. Guide him by the shore when the ocean shines like a silver mirror, or long white lines of breakers curl and

Spiritual Vision. 195

foam on the sands, or the billows, swelling as they roll and bursting with the roar of thunder, fling themselves in sheets of snow on the rugged cliffs; or lead him forth on a winter night, when a thousand stars are sparkling in the frosty sky; or take him on a summer day to the meadow carpeted with flowers of every form and the richest hues: he sees no wonders; not he! He only marvels at your admiration, and is disposed, as the world deals with those whose delight is in the word and service of God, to set you down for a hypocrite or a fanatic, a liar or a fool. You are neither. There are stars in heaven and flowers on earth. The man does not see them, because he is blind; and so are we, if we have no relish for the Word of God, nor see any gracious and glorious wonders there.

Open a blind man's eyes. With what amazement, admiration, happiness, overflowing joy will he gaze, nor tire gazing, on all above and around him, from the sun blazing in heaven to the tiniest flower that springs in beauty at his feet! And let God open a sinner's eyes, the Bible will seem to him a new book, and he seem to himself a new creature. Wonders! He will see his heart, and wonder at its wickedness. He will see the Saviour, and wonder at his love. He will see how God has spared him, and wonder at his long-suffering. He will see sin in its true colours, and wonder he could love a thing so vile and so detestable. He will see his own righteousness as treacherous sand, and wonder that he could have trusted to anything so bad. He will see salvation as the one thing needful, and wonder he could have taken a night's rest, ventured to close his eyes in sleep, till he had found peace with God. He will see the King in his transcendent beauty, and wonder, as he throws himself at Jesus's feet, that all the world does not do so—that all men do not go after him, saying, as he does, Jesus, thou art all my desire. Whom have I in heaven but thee? and there is none upon earth that I desire beside thee. Thou art chiefest among ten thousand, and altogether lovely!

IV. God only can open our eyes.

We need sight as well as light. Unless our eyes are opened, the Bible is of no more use to us than a lantern to a blind man in a dark night, and on a dangerous road—of no more use to us than a guide-book in Russian, Chinese, Arabic, or any other to us incomprehensible tongue—of no more use to us than the way-post, with painted finger pointing out the path to that blind beggar, who, with head erect and careful steps, comes on in the leading of a dog. To shew the pass, we raise *cairns* of weathered stones on our Highland hills, and when the way was lost, and hope with strength was sinking, as they caught sight of the rude pile looming through the mist, or rising black above the levelled snows, many have blessed the hands that raised the cairn; they owe their life to it. Abroad, among the Alps, Christianity there, modifying a custom older than itself, they substitute crosses for cairns; and where the road, leaving the gay and smiling valley, climbs into the realms of eternal winter, or is cut out of the face of precipices, down which one false step hurls the traveller into a gorge where the foaming torrent seems but a silver thread, tall crosses stand. And so, when the path is buried in the drift that spreads a treacherous crust over yawning crevice and deadly crag, he, by keeping the line of crosses, braves the tempest, and walks safely where otherwise it were death to venture. But set a blind man on such a road, and he never reaches home; the earth his bed and the snow his shroud, he sleeps the sleep that knows no waking. Now, there is a cross that points out man's way to heaven. But unless the eyes that sin sealed are open—have been opened by God to see it, and all the way-marks that mercy has set up to that happy home—our feet shall "stumble upon the dark mountains," and we shall perish for ever.

God only can do this. Hence to him David directs the prayer of my text; and also this—Lighten mine eyes, lest I sleep the sleep of death. Men use instruments to restore sight, and nowhere does surgery achieve a nobler triumph, or bestow greater blessings on mankind, than in yonder theatre, where skill and a steady hand, cut into the sightless balls; and man, opening a way for the light of heaven, imitates Christ in his divine works of might and mercy—pouring light into the blind man's eyes, and joy into the blind man's heart. God also uses instruments—his instrument the word, his agent the Holy Spirit. By these, working faith in men, and renewing them in the spirit of their minds, he has often answered, and is now ready to answer the prayer, Open thou mine eyes.

Let me illustrate the effect of this by three examples—

First, Look at Balaam. He is urging forward a restive and unwilling steed, as unconscious of danger as many who, in the pursuit of money or pleasure, are driving headlong on ruin. Wincing under its rider's blows, why will the beast not go forward? Why does she back and plunge? Balaam sees no danger ahead, nothing on the dusty path, but the flickering sunbeams, or the shadows of the vines that trail along the walls. What makes the obstinate, unruly brute run his limb against the wall, and bring down on its own head a shower of angry blows? Nothing that Balaam sees, till the Lord, as the Bible says, opened his eyes; and then and there, right in front of him, bestriding the narrow path, stands an angel, a sword glittering in his hand. And let God open a sinner's eyes, and how he would stare and tremble to see a sight more terrible—Justice, armed with the terrors of the law, barring his way to heaven. Learning, then, that by the deeds of the law no man living shall be justified, the poor soul gladly welcomes a despised, rejected Saviour, and falls at his feet, to cry, Lord, save me, I perish.

Secondly, Take a second case of divine illumination. A poor outcast, a wanderer in the thirsty desert, Hagar, whose sins have brought this misery on her head, has laid Ishmael down behind a bush to die. She can submit to her own death, but not see his; nor hear the cry, Water, mother, water! that comes faintly from his blackened lips. With nothing over her but a burning sun, nothing around her but glowing sands, and with the wind of that desert on her cheek like the breath of a fiery furnace, she retires out of earshot of Ishmael's moans, and sits down to die. In that hour of her extremity, of dark and deep despair, there comes a voice. She lifts her head, and, listening, hears it say, " What aileth thee, Hagar? fear not; for God hath heard the voice of the lad where he is. Arise, lift up the lad!"—and at the same moment there falls on her ear the blessed sound of bubbling water. God opens her eyes; and there a spring, inviting her to drink, is welling up from the burning sands. And let God open the eyes of any one who, amid terrors of conscience, feels ready to perish, and in the gospel, which before seemed so barren of pleasures, at the foot of the cross, and within his own soul, he will find "a well of water springing up into everlasting life."

Take another example. Alas, my master! how shall we do? is the cry of Elisha's servant, as he rushes into the house with pale terror in his face The Syrian host, by a forced night-march, has reached their city, encompassing it like a wall; and he has seen the morning sun glitter on swords, and spears, and the terrible array of war. Calm and self-possessed, his master answers, Fear not: for they that be with us are more than they that be with them. With us! the servant might ask,—who are with us? Where are they? The prophet prays, and in answer to his prayer, the Lord opens his servant's eyes. Now, as if they had started from the bowels of the earth, or every bush and every tree had suddenly changed into a flaming, celestial form, Behold, the mountain was full of horses and chariots of fire round about Elisha! And when memory has called up a believer's sins, and a sense of guilt has been darkening into despair, and Satan and his hosts, issuing from the pit, and drawn out in battle array, seem to have cut him off from escape, and he has been ready to cry, with Elisha's servant, Alas, my master, how shall I do? how has the Spirit of God flown to his help; and with eyes opened on the fulness, grace, mercy, pardon, and power we have in Jesus, how has he felt that, with God the Father, and God the Son, and God the Holy Spirit on his side, They that are with him are greater than all that can be against him.

XII.

THE APOSTATE.

"Demas hath forsaken me, having loved this present world."—
2 Tim. iv. 10.

IN old times our Nether Bow port and the gate of old London Bridge were often garnished with human heads; and on these, in days of tyranny and wrong, many a good, praying, and patriot head was spiked, alongside those of notorious criminals, to bake and wither in the sun. This, which we now consider a barbarous and offensive custom, was continued, after a fashion, down to our own age. Years ago, yet in our time, you could see, in sailing on the Thames, certain strange and fearful objects, close by the shore and standing up within tide-mark between you and the sky. They were gibbets, with dead men hung in chains. This spectacle, though repugnant to modern tastes and notions, had a good object in view; it accomplished something other and better than merely frightening those who, passing there by night, might hear the wind whistle through the holes of the empty skull, and the rusty chains creak as the body swayed round and round. Piracy, with its horrible atrocities on men and women, was then much more commonly practised by seamen than it is now, and as their ships dropped down the river, past these monuments of that crime and its punishment, the sailors carried away with them a salutary warning. They saw the abhorrence with which society regarded, and the vengeance with which justice pursued the perpetrators of so great a crime. Paul says, "Them that sin, rebuke before all, that others also may fear;" and these pirates were hung up before all for that good end. But the lesson, though striking, and well adapted, perhaps, to the rough men of rude times, was not perpetual. The work of decay went on, till bone dropping away from bone left only empty chains; and thus, mother earth hiding in her bosom the last relics of a guilty child, the criminal and his crime were both forgotten.

More enduring monuments than these of sin and of its punishment have perished amid the wrecks of time. For long ages, the stony form of a woman, dug from no quarry and cut by no sculptor's chisel, stood with its cold gray eyes turned on the sea that entombed the sinners but not the sin of Sodom. Lonely and awful figure, on her the traveller who skirted the shores of the Dead Sea, and shepherds tending their flocks on the neighbouring mountains, gazed with wonder and terror; and never did living preacher deliver such a sermon on the words, No man, having put his hand to the plough, and looking back, is fit for the kingdom of God, as that dumb statue. But time, the destroyer of all earthly things, has not spared even it; travellers have searched in vain for a relic more valuable and impressive far than the finest marbles of Greece and Rome. There is not a vestige of it to be found. She who, loving the present world too well, looked back on Sodom, has ceased to exist in stone, but she still lives in sacred story; and amid this world's temptations we would do well to think of and often to recall the words, "Remember Lot's wife."

The purpose which our ancestors had in view when they hung men in chains, and which God himself had in view when he turned Lot's wife into a pillar of salt, was St Paul's in his treatment of him whom he holds forth in this passage as a beacon to all future ages. He did not write these words to revenge himself on Demas, or to indulge any angry feeling against this poor and pitiable apostate. Nor was Demas the only man who had forsaken this champion of the truth. Stricken by such panic as has seized and scattered the bravest in battle, all Paul's companions deserted him at an awful crisis of affairs; and, referring to the scene where, with form bent beneath the weight of years and cares and labours, but spirit elastic and erect as ever, he stood alone at Nero's bar, he says, "At my first answer no man stood with me, but all men forsook me: I pray God that it may not be laid to their charge." But between these and Demas there was an essential difference, and now, they in heaven and he in hell, there is an eternal one. Recovering their courage, they rallied; and washed out in their own blood the stain of this disgrace. They fled the field for a time, he for ever; they abandoned the fight, he the faith; their conduct was a weakness, his was apostasy; theirs the failing of the disciples, for whom their Master offered the kind apology, "The spirit indeed is willing, but the flesh is weak," but his the crime and guilt of Judas. So, singling him out from the crowd, Paul, if I may so say, hangs the apostate up in chains. Recording the man's name and crime in these imperishable pages, he sets him before us to warn professing Christians against the love of the world; and teach all who, exposed to its influence and current, think they stand, to take heed lest they fall.

I. Let us consider the history and fall of Demas.

Men live after they are dead—some in their good deeds, others in their bad. Many a man would have been unheard of, but for his crimes; living but for these in happy obscurity, and going down to his grave unnoticed and unknown. But the case of Demas is not that of one who owes the world's only knowledge of him to his crimes, like a felon whom a scaffold raises above the heads of the vulgar crowd who have come to see him die. This is not the first time we hear of Demas; and, indeed, had St Paul written no second letter to Timothy, or had God in his providence been pleased to allow this epistle to perish with other writings of the apostles, Demas might have given a name to Protestant churches; he might have been sainted in the Romish calendar, and had devotees soliciting his prayers, while they burned candles and offered gifts at his shrine.

In falling, this man fell from a height which few have reached, and that makes his fall the more impressive—he was a fallen star. If to be praised, not by the common crowd, but by those who themselves are praised, is fame, if to be held up by those who stand on others' shoulders, is admitted to be the highest honour, such honour Demas had. Paul himself, the greatest of the apostles, once regarded him with warm affection, and awarded him the honour due to a fellow-labourer in the Lord. No common man at arms, he had stood in the front rank of the Christian host; and fighting in battle by the apostle's side, he had shared his dangers, and stood high in his esteem. Nor had he a place in Paul's heart only. He is made honourable mention of in his letters; in that to the Colossians, for instance, where the apostle joins Demas with one of the four Evangelists—"Luke," says he, "the beloved physician, and Demas greet you." We find him in no less honourable company also in that most touching letter to Philemon, where this lover of all freedom, and hater of all oppression, and denouncer of all human wrongs throws his arms around a slave as a brother beloved—breathing a spirit that, intolerant of slavery, would emancipate every bondman, and let the oppressed go free. "There salute thee," he says, "Epaphras, my fellow-prisoner in Christ Jesus; Marcus, Aristarchus, Demas, Lucas, my fellow-prisoners." What a galaxy of stars, and Demas shining among them! Names of renown, these sound in our ears like David's roll of mighty men; and the time was when Demas held such place among the champions of the cross, as, according to Scripture, belonged to Benaiah, the son of Jehoiada, who slew the lion-like men of Moab, and with no more formidable weapon than a staff encountered and conquered the Egyptian giant—" He was more honourable than the thirty, but he attained not to the first three."

Some men, as we might rashly say in our ignorance of the designs of Providence, die too soon; but some seem to live too long—outliving not their usefulness only, which, however undesirable, a good man may do, but their honour and principles. Happy for Demas had his sun gone down at noon! Over one who had been his friend, companion, fellow-labourer, with whom he had often taken sweet counsel, Paul lived to weep; and to write this epitaph for his un-honoured grave, Demas hath forsaken me, having loved this present world; a sentence that, like the scorpion, carries its sting in its tail,—" having loved this present world." Look at him! Ovid has fancied no metamorphosis more strange or horrible. The opposite of Paul, who fell a persecutor and rose an apostle, Demas, once an apostle, has changed into an apostate; once a martyr, now a renegade; a brave soldier once, now a base deserter; a traitor now; his arms raised to pull down the pillars of a church they had helped to build. May we not cry with the prophet, How art thou fallen from heaven, O Lucifer, son of the morning! Scripture is silent on this man's future course; the curtain falls where we see him as a dishonoured knight, with the spurs he had won hacked from his heels—as a deserter, with the facings plucked from his dress, and drummed out of the regiment. But if ancient tradition speaks truth, Demas, as might be expected, went from bad to worse, sank lower and lower, from one depth of wickedness to another; till he closed his infamous career as the priest of a heathen temple—offering sacrifices to dead stocks and stones. What a fall was there? Unhappy man! whether he died amid the recollections of other and better days, stung by remorse and howling in despair; or died in sullen defiance of the Saviour, like Julian, when, overcome in battle by the Christians, he caught the blood from his fatal wound, and, tossing it up in the face of heaven, cried, expiring in the effort, The Nazarene has conquered!

Such is the story of Demas. As instructive as it is sad. Let no man wonder now that John Bradford, living in a street along which criminals in his time were led to execution, was wont to say, as from his windows he saw them passing on to the gallows, But for the grace of God, there goes John Bradford! The fall of such an one as Demas, like some tall cliff which, undermined by the waves, precipitates itself with the roar of thunder headlong into the boiling sea, must have startled the Church at the time, and wakened from their slumber those that slept in Sion; and still, as if its echoes were yet sounding round the world, let us listen to its warning. It teaches the highest of us, to take heed lest we fall; the happiest of us, to rejoice with trembling; and all of us, to watch and pray that, keeping our garments unspotted from the world, we enter not into temptation.

II. Consider the cause of Demas' fall,—he loved this present world.

Sailing once along a Highland loch where the crag goes sheer down into the water, our attention was turned by the boatmen to an immense table of rock. Tilted up on its narrow edge, it stood there threatening destruction to any who ventured below it; appearing ready to topple over at the touch of an infant's finger, and leap with a sudden plunge into the bosom of the lake. How came this gigantic stone to assume that upright attitude? No brawny arms of shepherd lads had raised and balanced it there. No earthquake, rolling along those mountains, and turning its stroke upwards, as earthquakes sometimes do, had started this mass from its bed and poised it so. Nor had the lightning, leaping from its cloud on the mountain summits, struck the crag, and, splitting it, raised this giant fragment from its bed. That was the task of a much more quiet, feeble, simple, and secret agent. When Jehovah revealed himself to the prophet, it was not in the earthquake, or in the roaring hurricane, or in the blazing fire, but in a still, small voice; and the power that rent that solid rock, and raised the mass tottering on its narrow base, was of a kind as quiet, gentle, and unobtrusive. Borne on the wings of the autumn wind, or dropped by a passing bird, a little seed had fallen into a crevice of the rock. Sleeping the winter through, but finding shelter and congenial soil, it sprang with the spring; and fed by dews and rains, the tender shoot grew. In time it lifted up its head, and spread its branches above and its roots below—worming them into fissures, wrapping them round and round that stony table, which, as they grew and thickened, it raised slowly from its bed. And then, one day when the seedling had grown into a tree, a storm, acting on leafy branches that caught the wind like sails, turned that tree into a lever, and, heaving on the rock that had received the seed into its heart and the fatal embraces of its roots, raised the massy table from its bed and poised it on the edge of the dizzy crag; and there it stood erect, waiting another storm to be hurled into the mossy waters of that wild, dark mountain lake.

As that shall fall, so fell Demas from his lofty

place; so have many fallen; ay, and so, unless we are restrained and sustained by the grace of God, the best of us would fall. It is not the world, observe, nor its money, nor its honours, nor its enjoyments that the Bible condemns; but the love of them. Beware of that! At first it may seem little, small as a tiny seed, but let it get a lodgment within you, and, fed by indulgence, it grows there, so silently, perhaps, that while it is worming itself deeper in, and wrapping its strong roots round and round your heart, you may never suspect the hold it is getting of you. That appears when the hour of temptation comes, whatever form it may assume; and the man falls, to the astonishment of many, perhaps to his own. When persecution came upon the Church, how did it act on Demas? as the storm on the rock that had lodged the seed in its bosom, and which, but for the tree that sprang from it with wide-spread branches and embracing roots, had stood unmoved by tempests, let them blow their worst. Turning Demas into a beggar, casting him into prison, or bringing him to the scaffold, persecution might destroy what of wealth, pleasure, health, and life was his; but had he not loved them, allowed them to take root in his heart, and occupy the place that belonged to God, persecution had never destroyed him. Never; and when Paul the apostle stood with his gray head before the crowd that had assembled to see him die, Demas had been at his side; one chain of love, as of iron, binding them; as they had fought, they had fallen together; their blood had mingled in the same stream; their heads rolled on the same scaffold; one chariot had borne both martyrs to the skies; and over their mangled remains, carried by devout men to burial, a weeping church might have raised one monument to their memory—its inscription, these words of David, They "were lovely and pleasant in their lives, and in their death they were not divided."

It is another part of that lament which best suits this case of Demas—"How are the mighty fallen, and the weapons of war perished!" He was laid in an apostate's grave—not excepting a drunkard's, the most hopeless of any; and, ere we close it over him, let us, like soldiers marched at a military execution by the dead body of a comrade who has been shot for treachery, take a last look of this unhappy, guilty man. He loved the world; and what has it brought him to? what is that world to him now, for which he denied his Saviour and forsook his servants? what now profits him a world, for which he bartered his immortal soul? He was a preacher; nor the last who has turned back in the day of battle, and abandoned his principles when they had to be suffered for. He had been a preacher, perhaps an eloquent one; but he never preached a sermon such as he preaches now—himself the sermon, and these words his text, Love not the world, neither the things that are in the world. If any man love the world, the love of the Father is not in him.

III. Learn the lessons this case teaches.

Put not your trust in princes, says David, nor in preachers, says Demas—by his example. The ornament of the pulpit may become its disgrace; and He, who will not give his glory to another, may rebuke the idolatry of the people by shattering their idol, or, rather, by allowing the idol to shatter itself. On the very throne where Herod sat, arrayed in royal apparel, making an oration at which the people shouted, It is the voice of a god, and not of a man, the angel of the Lord smote him. His flatterers saw their god eaten up of worms. And what more excellent studies than he and Demas for any who are in danger of being intoxicated with popular applause, and of turning giddy from the height of their position? An apostle once, an apostate now; the object once of good men's affection, but now of bad men's contempt; once beloved by the Church, despised now even by the world, and, worse still, by himself; a blazing star quenched in night, how does Demas warn those who are high placed, not to be high-minded, but to fear. It is safest to carry a low sail in a strong wind, even when it blows in our favour. Blessed are the poor in spirit; for theirs is the kingdom of heaven. The humble are to be exalted; those who lie at Jesus' feet are those who shall lie on his bosom.

Then, again, what a lesson does Demas read such as, by their family circumstances, their pious friends, or otherwise, are placed in conditions the most favourable to their spiritual welfare? He associated with the holiest society out of heaven. The bosom friend of one in heart the purest, and in soul the loftiest, noblest man the world ever saw, and a fellow-labourer with him in the ministry of the gospel, Demas was in circumstances less likely than are any of us to get engrossed with the business, or burdened with the cares, or entangled with the pleasures of the world. Notwithstanding, he fell—drawn away by the love of the world from the love of Christ. And what need, then, have Christians much less favourably situated, to watch and pray, and guard their hearts? This story sounds in my ear like the voice of the old prophet, "Howl, fir-tree; for the cedar is fallen."

Do you feel at ease, considering yourselves in small danger of suffering such persecutions as led to the fall of Demas? It may be so; but let me warn you that the world has trials more testing and severe than these. Its smiles are to be dreaded, perhaps, more than its frowns, its subtle sophistries more than its sharpest sword. Let its love but once get into a man's heart, and it has a tongue to persuade him that vice is virtue, and virtue vice. Look at the sentiments of such as make a profession of religion, and yet love the world —fearing the Lord, and serving their own gods. According to them, a stern regard to duty, integrity, purity, is preciseness, and the holy observance of God's day is Pharisaism;—on the other hand, conformity to the fashions and practices and gaieties of the world is not being "righteous overmuch;" a godless indifference to religious matters is charity and catholicity; looseness of principle is liberality, and freedom from the trammels of sectarianism; flattery and fawning are politeness, or, to profane the Scripture expression, are to be courteous; low cunning is caution; cowardice in the cause of God and truth is prudence; treachery to public principle is a wise regard to our own interests; dishonesty and fraud are cleverness in business; murder is an affair of honour, and seduction one of gallantry; hoarding money is carefulness; and the avarice that eats like a cancer into the heart, destroying alike the love of God and the love of man, is such frugality as Christ commended, and, indeed, commanded, when he said, Gather up the fragments that remain, that nothing be lost. And thus, when the love of the world has entered our hearts, the devil, clothed like an angel of light, walks in at its back.

In old times the sailors, a race given to superstition, told among other stories of the sea one of a strange island that lay in waters where no breakers beat, nor storms blew on its quiet shores. Yet they give it a wide berth whenever they, as they supposed, approached its neighbourhood, holding it in greater dread than the rugged coasts of our stormy climes. It rose from the deep a mass of magnetic ore, with powers of attraction fatal to the mariner. Once within their influence, the ship was drawn nearer and nearer; at first slowly, silently, gently, almost imperceptibly, but with ever-increasing speed; till, on a close approach, every iron bolt drawn from her timbers, without a crash, or sound, or anything to alarm the waking, or to wake the sleeping, she fell into a thousand pieces; and the whole fabric dissolved, crew and cargo sank together—down into that quiet sea. Fable as that was, so goes the religion, such as it is, of him who, drawn to the world, yields up his heart to its fatal attractions. It draws him on and on, further and faster on, till at length the catastrophe arrives—his principles give way before some great temptation, and he is lost. What a wreck it made of Demas!

Watch, therefore, and pray while you watch, against this insidious enemy. If you find yourself beginning to love any pleasure better than your prayers—any book better than your Bible—any house better than God's—any table better than the Lord's—any person better than your Saviour—any one better than your soul—a present indulgence better than the hopes of heaven—take alarm. The evil is begun, and it does not mend the matter that its beginning is small. It does not need a large hole to admit a serpent with poison in its fangs, nor a large leak to let in the water that sinks the ship and drowns her crew. Despise not the day of small things, be they for good or evil. Behold, how great a matter a little fire kindleth! Beware how you allow Satan, or any one else, to lodge the love of the world in the smallest cranny or crevice of your heart. Give your hands to the world, but keep your heart for God. It is a very good world if kept in its own place; like fire and water, a useful servant, but a bad and most tyrannous master. Love it not, and yet love it. Love it with the love of him who gave his Son to die for it. Love it with the love of him who shed his blood to save it. Love it with the love of angels, who rejoice in its conversion. Love it to do it good, giving your tears to its sufferings—your pity to its sorrows—your wealth to its wants—your prayers to its miseries—and to its fields of charity and philanthropy and Christian piety, your powers and hours of labour. You cannot live without affecting it, or being affected by it. You will make the world better, or it will make you worse. God help you by his grace and Holy Spirit so to live in the world as to live above it, and look beyond it; and so to love it, that when you leave it, and the fluttering heart has beat its last stroke, and the bosom has heaved its last long sigh, and the last quiver has passed from your lips, and no breath dims the mirror, and all is over, you may leave the world better than you found it!

THE END.

Ballantyne and Company, Printers, Edinburgh.

BOOKS FOR THE PEOPLE.

Now in course of Publication,

STRAHAN'S FAMILY LIBRARY

OF

BOOKS AT ONCE CHEAP, VALUABLE, AND INSTRUCTIVE.

In Crown 8vo Volumes, printed on Toned Paper, and Elegantly Bound, Price 3s. 6d. each.

All that the Publishers wish to say, by way of Prospectus, is, that their aim in this Library is not ignobly to interest, or frivolously to amuse, but to convey the wisest instruction in the pleasantest manner. They desire, in short, to produce a series of Books which will not only be worth reading, but will be worth keeping, and which will find their way to tens of thousands of British homes, to be well thumbed and dog-eared by the children and the grown people, on the journey and at the fireside.

The following are a few of the Books which will be earliest issued:—

I.

THE RECREATIONS OF A COUNTRY PARSON.

Originally published in FRASER'S MAGAZINE.

II.

SPEAKING TO THE HEART.

BY THOMAS GUTHRIE, D.D.,
Author of "A Plea for Ragged Schools," "The Gospel in Ezekiel," &c.

III.

PARISH PAPERS:
PERSONAL, SOCIAL, AND CONGREGATIONAL.

By NORMAN MACLEOD, D.D.,
Of the Barony Parish, Glasgow.

IV.

PRAYING AND WORKING;
BEING SOME ACCOUNT OF WHAT MEN CAN DO WHEN IN EARNEST.

By WILLIAM FLEMING STEVENSON.

V.

TRAVELS IN THE SERVICE OF SCIENCE.

By Professor C. PIAZZI SMYTH,
Astronomer-Royal for Scotland,
Author of "Three Cities of Russia," "The Peak of Teneriffe," &c.

VI.

THE HOUSEHOLD HYMNS OF GERMANY AND THE NORTH.

Edited and Translated under the direction of Miss GREENWELL,
Author of "The Patience of Hope."

VII.

THE GRAVER THOUGHTS OF A COUNTRY PARSON.

By the Author of "Recreations of a Country Parson."

VIII.

SUBURBAN:

A BOOK OF ESSAYS WRITTEN IN THE COUNTRY.

By ALEXANDER SMITH,

Secretary to the University of Edinburgh; Author of "The Life Drama," "City Poems," &c.

IX.

A POPULAR EDITION OF

THE EARNEST STUDENT;

BEING MEMORIALS OF JOHN MACKINTOSH.

By NORMAN MACLEOD, D.D.,
Of the Barony Parish, Glasgow.

X.

NEW LIFE IN THE PARISH:

A RECORD OF ENCOURAGING EXPERIENCES.

By the Rev. Dr BÜCHSEL, Berlin.

In Two Vols., Crown 8vo, Price 12s.,

THE OLD LIEUTENANT AND HIS SON.

BY NORMAN MACLEOD, D.D.,
ONE OF HER MAJESTY'S CHAPLAINS FOR SCOTLAND.

EXTRACT FROM PREFACE.

"Why should a man, who is 'some fifty,' apologise to the public for beginning to tell stories? Is not this a very common phenomenon 'at his time of life?' I have, indeed, no good reason to give for writing this tale, except one,—which, after all, is no reason, but the mere statement of a fact, whatever be *its* reason,—viz., that I could not help it! When I began to write about the Old Lieutenant, it was my intention merely to occupy a chapter or two of *Good Words* with a life-sketch drawn from memories of the past. But the sketch grew upon me. Persons and things and scenes came crowding out of the darkness; and while I honestly wished to mould them for practical good, I felt all the while more possessed by them than possessing them. My own half-creations became my tyrants; and so I was driven on, and on, from chapter to chapter, until, fortunately for myself, and much more for my readers, the end of the volume, and the end of the year, forced me to stop.

"Having taken, however, the first bold step of publishing the story in *Good Words*, the second which I now take, of publishing it separately, can hardly make matters better or worse for me. The fact of an unauthorised edition being issued in America, confirms me in the resolution to publish a corrected one here.

"I have only further to state, that as the story was written and published month after month, amidst the more grave and heavier labours of a large parish, a few changes are made, which would have been unnecessary had it been first written as a whole before publication.

"With these explanations, I send 'The Old Lieutenant and his Son' once more on their voyage. May they do evil to no man, but do good to many!"

Twenty-Seventh Thousand.

Now Ready, in Gilt Cloth, Antique, Price 3s. 6d.,

THE NEAR AND THE HEAVENLY HORIZONS.

By the COUNTESS DE GASPARIN.

" Earth by Heaven, and Heaven by changeful Earth, Illustrated and mutually endeared."—*Wordsworth.*

"This is a charming book. Madame de Gasparin has the touch of genius which has the strange gift of speaking to every one 'in their own tongue.'"—*Athenæum.*

"'The Near and the Heavenly Horizons' is a book full of beauty and pathos."—*British Quarterly Review.*

"Be persuaded, reader, to get this beautiful volume. It is just the book for Sabbath afternoons in a Christian family."—*Eclectic Review.*

"The pictures of nature here are wondrous. This book speaks to the hearts of us all."—*Macmillan's Magazine.*

"This is by far the ablest book that has yet appeared on the subject of the life after death. Never before have we seen such irresistible arguments for THE ETERNITY OF LOVE, and THE REUNION OF FAMILIES IN HEAVEN."—*Caledonian Mercury.*

"These pages are like gossamer threads beaded with radiant dew-drops. . . . . The book is one which ought to become extremely popular."—*The Witness.*

"Let us say at once of 'The Near and the Heavenly Horizons,' that we have scarcely ever read a book with more enjoyment than its perusal has afforded us."—*Aberdeen Free Press.*

"A remarkable book—displaying marvellous powers of descriptive writing."—*The Scotsman.*

"This is a book to be enjoyed and revelled in rather than criticised. The reader who sits down to it will have a rare literary treat."—*The Scottish Guardian.*

"This is the most charming book of the year, without any qualification. It is impossible to write of it as of an ordinary volume. It carries the reader away—so enthusiastic, so true, so faithful, so natural is it."—*The Standard.*

"This book is poetry in prose, in very deed. We have seldom met with a more delicious volume. The authoress carries a perfect witchery in her pen."—*The London Quarterly Review.*

TENTH THOUSAND
is Now Ready of

HEALTH: Five Lay Sermons to Working People.

BY JOHN BROWN, M.D.,

AUTHOR OF "RAB AND HIS FRIENDS."

In Neat Cloth, Price 1s.

STRAHAN & Co. beg to announce that the Five Lay Sermons forming the above work will shortly be issued at 1d. each, in the following order:—

I. OUR DUTY TO THE DOCTOR.
II. THE DOCTOR'S DUTY TO US.
III. CHILDREN; AND HOW TO GUIDE THEM.
IV. HEALTH.
V. MEDICAL ODDS AND ENDS.

"A racy, eloquent, colloquial talk to working people about the doctor, the management of children, and the preservation of health, worthy of being put side by side with Miss Nightingale's 'Notes on Nursing.'"—*The Patriot.*

"In a fine, racy, homely way, Dr Brown conveys a vast store of practical wisdom on the manner of preserving health and preventing disease, both in children and adults. If working men—and others even who are not called working men—would but read these 'Lay Sermons,' and act upon their precepts, how much less misery should we have in the world!"—*Aberdeen Herald.*

"In his powerful and clear and beautifully simple way, the Doctor gives the people much valuable counsel on the question of health and its preservation. It is surprising how much wisdom he puts into so little room, and with what words of kindness and what telling anecdotes—these drawn from his own experience—he makes this little medical work as interesting as if it were a powerfully written romance. Need we say more to commend the book to our readers? Not we. The Doctor's name is a household word, and this, his latest volume, will soon be in the hands of the tens of thousands of the admirers of 'Rab and his Friends.'"—*Dundee Advertiser.*

The Third Edition will shortly be Ready of

PAPERS FOR THOUGHTFUL GIRLS:
WITH
ILLUSTRATIVE SKETCHES OF SOME GIRLS' LIVES.

By SARAH TYTLER.

ILLUSTRATED BY J. E. MILLAIS.

In Crown 8vo, price 5s.

" . . . This book is worthy of a place in the library of every family."—*The Daily News.*

"It is many a day since we read a book that has gratified us more than Miss Tytler's. Her perfect womanliness—her intuitive sagacity—her homely good sense—her natural unaffected piety—her thoughtful pictorial style, make her book a most valuable companion. Happy would it be for our girls if they would mould their characters and consecrate their gifts according to it. What sisters, and wives, and mothers we should have! And yet not an extravagant word is to be found in it—all is plain, practical good sense. This, indeed, is the charm of her book. She discourses about youth, intellect, beauty, friendship, love, godliness, &c., with the practical purpose, wise discrimination, and rich thoughtfulness of Archbishop Whately or Lord Bacon: and then she does what neither of our great ethical philosophers could have done—tells an admirable story illustrative of her theme."—*Evangelical Magazine.*

"This modest and suggestive work deserves to be widely known. Such a wholesome blending of unconditional freedom with womanly delicacy, of practical good sense with warm human sympathy and religious idealism, is as rare as it is wholesome. We commend the book to all young ladies, wishing the half of the novels of the day were as wholesome and suggestive as these 'Papers for Thoughtful Girls.'"—*The Economist.*

"One of the most fascinating books we have ever seen for the rising youth of the fair sex. The whole volume is so lively, and yet so serious, that we would disclaim all liking for the young lady who should not fall in love with it."—*Eclectic Review.*

"Here we have one of the best books that ever was written for a purpose. There has recently been no lack of books on the whole duty of women; but in none of them has there been so catholic a spirit, so just an appreciation of all the adornments of the feminine character."—*The Scotsman.*

"One of the most charming books of its class that we have ever read. It is even superior to Miss Mulock's well-known work 'A Woman's Thoughts about Women.' It is just such a book as we should select to place in the hands of a sister or a daughter upon her entrance into life, to guide her in danger, and counsel her in difficulty, to lead her upwards and onwards, and to shew her what her duty is here, and her happiness hereafter. Miss Tytler has produced a work which will be popular in many a home when her name has become among her own friends nothing more than a memory."—*The Morning Herald.*

Fifth Thousand will shortly be Ready, Crown 8vo, 3s. 6d.,

BEGINNING LIFE.

CHAPTERS FOR YOUNG MEN ON RELIGION, STUDY, AND BUSINESS.

By JOHN TULLOCH, D.D.,
Principal and Primarius Professor, St Mary's College, St Andrews.

"It is gratifying to see one whose office connects him so closely with the intellectual and religious interests of the country, and whose name is now so well and widely known, coming forth to address a larger audience of young men than he can gather in his own class-room, and speaking to them frankly and faithfully about the great religious truths which he believes lie at the root of all excellence in life. He speaks as a friend to friends, with hearty sympathy for every difficulty, and with a clear insight of the truth that will resolve the difficulty."—*The Scotsman.*

"To this volume we give the highest praise. Principal Tulloch is no mere philosopher. He brings his subject down to young men's business and bosoms. We hope that our wealthier readers will put this volume into the hands of many young men who could not otherwise procure it. It is a book that will well sustain the reputation of its author."—*The Baptist Magazine.*

"This is in every way a masterly performance—well calculated to strengthen and elevate the mind. There is not a feeble or flimsy chapter in the volume. It is beaten gold throughout."—*The Christian Witness.*

"A book largely imbued with warm religious principle, and a deep-toned, out-spoken, healthy charity. We know no more fitting book for youths about to enter on the battle of life."—*The Morning Journal.*

"This is a work written by one whose youthful sympathies are still lively, and whose academical position eminently qualifies him to know what is passing in the minds of the rising generation, and how they may be most effectually influenced."—*The Dundee Advertiser.*

"As a book for young men, it is vastly superior to any we have ever seen."—*The Glasgow Herald.*

32 LUDGATE HILL, LONDON.

WORKS BY HORACE BUSHNELL, D.D.

I.
NATURE AND THE SUPERNATURAL,
AS TOGETHER CONSTITUTING THE ONE SYSTEM OF GOD.

Fourth Thousand. Crown 8vo, Price 3s. 6d.

"We have not had in our hands for a long time a book from which so many beautiful and powerful passages could be selected. . . . The book is a remarkable one, and deserves to be widely known and read."—*The British Quarterly Review.*

"To thoughtful and open and candid minds this will be a priceless volume."—*The Eclectic Review.*

"Though this is a great book, for such we deem it, it is not an obscure, still less a dull one. It will prove intensely interesting to every intelligent reader."—*Scottish Congregational Magazine.*

II.
THE NEW LIFE.
Fifteenth Thousand. Crown 8vo, 4s. 6d. Cheap Edition, 1s. 6d.

"Of all the books published in recent years with a view to promote personal holiness, we most value and admire Dr Bushnell's 'New Life.'"—*New York Independent.*

"A volume of profound thought and splendid eloquence. It displays the author's great powers in their happiest and most useful exercise."—*Edinburgh Courant.*

"No discourses recently published in this country have any claim to be ranked with Dr Bushnell's, except, perhaps, those of Robertson of Brighton, and, though at a considerable distance, those of John Caird. It were indeed a high day for the Church, if its ministry acquired the tone and rose to the power which this book reveals."—*Dundee Advertiser.*

"We have here a Christian preacher dealing with some of the profoundest themes of Christian experience, with an insight into the working of the human soul, a grasp and breadth of thought, and a depth of experience, such as we have never seen equalled. The soul of the reader of this volume comes into vital contact with another soul which has reflected deeply on life's great problems, has suffered in life's struggles, and found a healing balm in Christ's work, and repose in communion with God."—*The Patriot.*

III.
CHRISTIAN NURTURE;
OR, THE GODLY UPBRINGING OF CHILDREN.

Fifth Thousand. Crown 8vo, 1s. 6d.

IV.
THE CHARACTER OF JESUS.
Twentieth Thousand. Neat Cloth, Red Edges, 6d.

WORKS BY HENRY WARD BEECHER.

I.
ROYAL TRUTHS.
Sixth Thousand. Crown 8vo, Red Edges, 3s. 6d.

"To any one who has read 'Life Thoughts,' by the same author, it will be enough to state the title of this work to secure for it an immediate perusal. Every home will be made the brighter and happier by having these 'Royal Truths' for perusal and consideration. There is vitality in the book, and every page of it will do some reader good. Here are truths to cheer, truths to comfort, truths to encourage, truths to guide, truths to instruct, truths for the young, truths for the old, truths to warn, truths to admonish, truths to build up believers, and some truths suited to every condition in life."—*Wesleyan Times.*

"Mr Beecher's name has become a household word. No American name is so familiar to the religious people of England. No one, perhaps, deserves to be so. For fresh and vivid conceptions, combined with the effective utterance of truth, no man can be compared with him. . . . To those who like a fresh dewy thought to lay upon their heart in the morning, or to lay upon a friend's heart, we heartily commend this vigorous and healthy book."—*The Patriot.*

"We know no modern book possessed of greater stimulating powers than this one, or that brings home to a healthy mind truths of greater freshness and beauty. In our opinion, it is even superior to the author's 'Life Thoughts;' and without doubt it will equal, if not go far beyond it in circulation."—*Caledonian Mercury.*

"This work is happily named. It is indeed a book brimful of burning, brilliant, beautiful 'Royal Truths,' each one more powerfully practical than another, and all combining to render the work one of the most remarkable for practical lessons, suggestive thoughts, scriptural ideas, and thoroughly evangelical sentiments that has appeared in this age of book writing."—*The Northern Ensign.*

"He is the benefactor in the present day who can, from whatever quarter, by whatever artillery, lodge a sufficient number of hot and living truths in the hearts of men. Now Henry Ward Beecher is precisely the man for this, and the present form of publication is precisely the way for his doing it. For of this book it may be said with much truth what Tennyson says of the poet:—

'He gives the people of his best:
His worst he kept; his best he gave.'

Among living writers, there is perhaps no *skirmisher* equal to Mr Beecher."—*The News of the Churches.*

"Thousands of our readers have read and rejoiced in Henry Ward Beecher's 'Life Thoughts,' and they will buy eagerly this companion volume. It is in no way inferior to its predecessor. In every page there is an exuberance of fresh, beautiful, living thought; and the reading of the book by snatches (which is obviously the way to read it) is like a trip to the Lakes or the Highlands. The reader is made a healthier, happier, better man."—*Glasgow Morning Journal.*

II.

LIFE THOUGHTS.
Fortieth Thousand.
Neat Cloth Antique, 2s. 6d.

"Every page is covered with sentences full of life—rich, deep, strong, beautiful. You will search in it vainly for aught that's dull. The facility of illustration manifested is marvellous. Knowledge, imagination, shrewdness, and piety are admirably blended. Taking this book as a whole, we can only say the like of it will not soon occur again, unless we have more of Beecher's Life Thoughts."—*Evangelical Magazine.*

"They are pregnant with celestial fire, rich in suggestive and original thought. Here we find nuggets of gold and gems of the first water..... Beecher is not a model, but he is better—he is capital, available capital on which others may draw, and send what they draw into currency in thoughts and words that will do the world a vast deal of good."—*London Press.*

"These are truly 'Life Thoughts.' They have the breath of life in them, and are strikingly original and memorable. They are sparks struck off from a mind of rare powers, and we are mistaken if they do not retain a permanent place in our literature."—*From the Congregational Magazine.*

"Here are 400 pages of the wisest, deepest, and most striking utterances, by one of the most original, brilliant, and versatile minds of the age. There is more philosophy here in some single pages than many an elaborate treatise contains; more religious stimulus than in a score of bepraised sermons; more poetry than in some acres of careful rhyming."
—*From the Baptist Quarterly.*

III.

SUMMER IN THE SOUL.
Sixth Thousand.
Neat Cloth Antique, 2s. 6d.

WORKS BY DORA GREENWELL.

I.

In Foolscap 8vo, Price 6s.,

CHRISTINA, AND OTHER POEMS.

Dr JOHN BROWN, (Author of "Rab and his Friends,") in "North British Review."

"Here is a poet as true as George Herbert or Henry Vaughan or our own Cowper. There is a personality and immediateness, a sort of sacredness and privacy, as if they were overheard rather than read, which gives to these remarkable productions a charm and a flavour all their own. With no effort, no consciousness of any end but that of uttering the inmost thoughts and desires of the heart, they flow out as clear, as living, as gladdening, as the wayside well—coming from out the darkness of the central depths, filtered into purity by time and travel. The waters are copious, sometimes to overflowing; but they are always limpid and unforced, singing their own quiet tune, not saddening, though sometimes sad, and their darkness—not that of obscurity but of depth—like that of the deep sea. We advise our readers to possess the book, and get the joy and the surprise of so much real thought and feeling. It is a *cardiphonia* set to music."

THE ATHENÆUM.

"Miss Greenwell is specially endowed as a writer of sacred poetry; and it is the rarest realm of all with the fewest competitors for its crown. She seems to us to be peculiarly fitted with natural gifts for entering into the chambers of the human heart, and to be spiritually endowed to walk there, with a brightening influence, cheering, soothing, exalting with words of comfort and looks of love, as a kind of Florence Nightingale walking the hospital of ailing souls."

THE NONCONFORMIST.

"Amongst volumes of verse lately given to the world, none has truer and richer poetic qualities than this. The authoress must be ranked with genuine poets, and her poems will bring good and soothingness to the hearts of her readers. We bend a grateful ear to this music, and we take the singer to our hearts."

II.

Second Edition, in Small Octavo, Price 2s. 6d.,

THE PATIENCE OF HOPE.

"This is the most thoughtful and suggestive book of our day."—*The Witness.*

"This beautiful book of Christian meditations is worthy of all praise; for, like all true, simple, natural things, there is in it a beauty and charm quite inexpressible. You must come away from looking into it, for your heart has no mirror clear and deep enough to draw forth and make your own all its radiance and aroma, and you must leave unappropriated much that seems most graceful, and tender, and sacred. A true book it is, we have said; and to say this is to put it out of the range of mere praise; for all true words about such things awaken in the hearer rather delight in the truth they utter, and wonder because of its infinite beauty, than incite to praise and eulogy. . . . . This is a book for Christian men; for the quiet hour of holy solitude, when the heart longs and waits for access to the presence of the Master. The weary heart that thirsts amidst its conflicts and its toils for refreshing water, will drink eagerly of these sweet and refreshing words. To thoughtful men and women, especially such as have learnt any of the patience of hope in the experiences of sorrow and trial, we commend this little volume most heartily and earnestly."—*The Scottish Press.*

"We cannot express the pleasure with which we have read this exquisitely-written book. . . . . It is conceived in the spirit of a meditative philosophy, irradiated through and through by the golden light of Christian feeling."—*The News of the Churches.*

"A work of singular philosophic power, as well as poetic beauty."— *Family Treasury.*

"Our admiration of the searching, fearless speculation, the wonderful power of speaking clearly upon dark and all but unspeakable subjects, the rich outcome of 'thoughts that wander through eternity,' increases every time we take up this wonderful little book."—*The North British Review.*

III.

Third Edition, in Small Octavo, Price 2s. 6d.,

A PRESENT HEAVEN.

"The production of a thoughtful, cultivated Christian mind, setting forth in great fulness and beauty the present privileges of the believer." —*Baptist Magazine.*

IV.

Shortly will be Published, in Small Octavo,

THE TWO FRIENDS.

V.

Preparing for Publication,

OUR SINGLE WOMEN.

REPRINTED FROM THE "NORTH BRITISH REVIEW," WITH NUMEROUS ADDITIONS AND ALTERATIONS.

ALEXANDER STRAHAN & CO.,

FORTIETH THOUSAND
is Now Ready of
THE PATHWAY OF PROMISE;
OR,
WORDS OF COMFORT TO THE CHRISTIAN PILGRIM.

In Neat Cloth Antique, Price 1s. 6d.

Uniform with the above—

THE NINTH THOUSAND
is Now Ready of
PERSONAL PIETY:
A HELP TO CHRISTIANS TO WALK WORTHY OF THEIR CALLING.

In Neat Cloth Antique, Price 1s. 6d.

Uniform with the above—

Now Ready,

SONGS FROM A SICK CHAMBER.
By the late H. MARY T.

In Neat Cloth Antique, Price 1s. 6d.

Uniform with the above—

Now Ready,

AIDS TO PRAYER.

In Neat Cloth Antique, Price 1s. 6d.

Uniform with the above—

Now Ready,

THE SUNDAY-EVENING BOOK

OF PAPERS FOR FAMILY READING, BY

JAMES HAMILTON, D.D.	Rev. W. M. PUNSHON.
Canon STANLEY.	JOHN EADIE, LL.D., D.D.
Rev. THOMAS BINNEY.	J. R. MACDUFF, D.D.

In Neat Cloth Antique, Price 1s. 6d.

Uniform with the above—

Preparing for Publication,

A NEW WORK

BY THE AUTHOR OF "THE PATHWAY OF PROMISE."

In Neat Cloth Antique, Price 1s. 6d.

Uniform with the above—

Preparing for Publication,

SHORT PAPERS ON GREAT SUBJECTS.

In Neat Cloth Antique, Price 1s. 6d.

Uniform with the above—

Preparing for Publication,

FELLOWSHIP WITH JESUS.

In Neat Cloth Antique, Price 1s. 6d.

Uniform with the above—

Preparing for Publication,

THE SINNER'S WELCOME.

In Neat Cloth Antique, Price 1s. 6d.

Sixth Thousand. Fine Edition, 5s. Cheap Edition, 2s. 6d.

THE GOLD THREAD.

A STORY FOR THE YOUNG.

By NORMAN MACLEOD, D.D., one of her Majesty's Chaplains for Scotland, Author of "Wee Davie," "The Earnest Student," &c., &c.

Illustrated in the highest style of Art, by J. D. WATSON, GOURLAY STEELL, and J. MACWHIRTER.

From the Caledonian Mercury.

"This is one of the prettiest as it is one of the best children's books in the language. Dr Macleod is great as a preacher and writer, but he is nowhere so great as in the field of nursery literature. Wherever there are children, if our advice is taken, there will be a GOLD THREAD. It is impossible to give any idea of the book by extracts, but we cannot refrain from quoting *The Squirrel's Song*, which stamps Dr Macleod a true poet. As little Eric, the hero of the story, lies at the foot of a gigantic tree, he thinks he hears, in his half-waking dream, a little squirrel sing this song:—

'I'm a merry, merry squirrel,
All day I leap and whirl,
Through my home in the old beech-tree;
If you chase me, I will run
In the shade and in the sun,
But you never, never can catch me!
For round a bough I'll creep,
Playing hide-and-seek so sly,
Or through the leaves bo-peep,
With my little shining eye.
Ha, ha, ha! ha, ha, ha! ha, ha, ha!

'Up and down I run and frisk,
With my bushy tail to whisk
All who mope in the old beech-trees;
How droll to see the owl,
As I make him wink and scowl,
When his sleepy, sleepy head I tease!
And I waken up the bat,
Who flies off with a scream,
For he thinks that I'm the cat
Pouncing on him in his dream.
Ha, ha, ha! ha, ha, ha! ha, ha, ha!

'Through all the summer long
I never want a song
From my birds in the old beech-trees,
I have singers all the night,
And with the morning bright
Come my busy humming fat brown bees.
When I've nothing else to do,
With the nursing birds I sit,
And we laugh at the cuckoo
A-cuckooing to her tit:
Ha, ha, ha! ha, ha, ha! ha, ha, ha!

'When winter comes with snow,
And its cruel tempests blow
All the leaves from my old beech-trees,
Then beside the wren and mouse
I furnish up a house,
Where like a prince I live at my ease!
What care I for hail or sleet,
With my hairy cap and coat;
And my tail across my feet,
Or wrapp'd about my throat!
Ha, ha, ha! ha, ha, ha! ha, ha, ha!'"

32 LUDGATE HILL, LONDON.

The Sixth Thousand is Now Ready,
In Crown 8vo, Price 3s. 6d. Cloth,

THE WORDS OF THE ANGELS;
OR, THEIR VISITS TO THE EARTH, AND THE MESSAGES THEY DELIVERED.

By RUDOLPH STIER, D.D., Author of "The Words of the Risen Saviour."

CONTENTS.

PART I.—THE HISTORICAL BOOKS.

1. Gabriel's Announcement to Zacharias.
2. Gabriel's Announcement to Mary.
3. Appearance of the Angel in a Dream to Joseph.
4. The Angels that Announce the Birth of Christ at Bethlehem.
5. The Angel returns to Joseph in Dreams.
6. The Angels at the Sepulchre.
7. The Angel's Question to Magdalene.
8. The Angels at the Ascension.
9. The Angel Opening the Prison Doors.
10. The Angel directing Philip.
11. The Angel sent to Cornelius.
12. The Angel delivering Peter.
13. The Angel to Paul at Sea.

PART II.—THE REVELATION OF ST JOHN.

14. The Praise of the Four Living Creatures.
15. Who is Worthy to Open the Book?
16. The Praise of many Angels, and the Amen of the Four Living Creatures.
17. The Fourfold Call—Come and See.
18. The Angel having the Seal for the Servants of God.
19. The Worship of all the Angels.
20. The Threefold Woe.
21. The Angel with the Little Book Open.
22. The Three Angels that Herald the Fall of Babylon.
23. The Two Angels at the Thrusting in of the Sickles.
24. The Angel of the Waters Praises God's Justice.
25. The Angel who shews the Mystic Babylon.
26. The Two Angels at the Fall of Babylon.
27. The Angel refusing to be Worshipped.
28. The Angel in the Sun summoning the Birds to the Great Supper.
29. The Great Voice out of Heaven.
30. The Interposing Voice.
31. The Angel shewing the Bride.
32. The last Angelic Speech.

The Journal of Sacred Literature.
"This work is one which will be read with pleasure and profit by every pious person. We have ourselves been much gratified with its perusal."

The Nonconformist.
"A very interesting volume by one of the most spiritual and suggestive of biblical expositors. It cannot be more highly praised than in saying, that it has the best characteristics of the author's universally-prized work on 'The Words of the Lord Jesus.'"

The Patriot.
"'The Words of the Angels' is full of just and beautiful thought. Each narrative of angelic communication is carefully and beautifully expounded, and its meaning and lessons pointed out. The book is one with which every devout reader will be charmed."

ALEXANDER STRAHAN & CO.,

The Fourth Thousand is Now Ready, in Square 8vo, Price 3s. 6d. Cloth, with Sixteen full-page Illustrations,

THE POSTMAN'S BAG:
A STORY-BOOK FOR BOYS AND GIRLS.

By the Rev. J. DE LIEFDE, Amsterdam,
Author of "The Pastor of Gegenburg."

"John de Liefde is a man whom to know is to admire and love. This little volume is like its writer—simple, artless, and Christian. We know several little children who are never weary of these little stories, and we are sure that they can learn from them nothing but what is good."—*London Review.*

"This is perhaps one of the best books for juveniles we have seen, and one which every family of young children will be much the better of possessing. It inculcates the principles of Christianity under the garb of pleasing tales and fables. We have no doubt it will cause many a face to beam with delight on receiving it from paterfamilias' hand. There are numerous excellent full-page illustrations by some of the best artists. 'The Postman's Bag' and the 'Golden Cap,' the first and the last of the series, are the best, but the interest of the young reader will be kept up *ab ovo usque ad mala.* The book is beautifully got up."—*Aberdeen Herald.*

"Commend us to Mr Liefde for a pleasant story, whether in the parlour or on the printed page. He is himself a story-book, full of infectious humour, racy anecdote, youthful freshness, and warm-hearted religion. In this pretty little volume we do not get any of his more elaborate tales; it is professedly a book 'for boys and girls,' and is made up of short stories and fables, the very things to win children's hearts."—*The Patriot.*

"'The Postman's Bag' is really a handsome juvenile volume. It is got up in the most attractive manner; its illustrations are executed with admirable taste; the paper, type, and binding are equally beautiful, and the stories are just the thing for the young folks, many of whom will revel in its pages with unceasing delight. The moral of all the stories is sound and salutary."—*Northern Ensign.*

THE SECOND THOUSAND

is Now Ready of

CHRISTIAN BELIEVING AND LIVING.

By F. D. HUNTINGTON, D.D.

In Crown 8vo, Price 3s. 6d.

"A year ago Dr Huntington was a distinguished Socinian preacher, and a Professor in the very celebrated, but very latitudinarian, University of Harvard; he is now, in the evangelical sense of the title, *a minister of the gospel* in connexion with the Episcopal Church. If among the 'remarkable conversions' of the present day we were permitted to chronicle that of James Martineau, and if he, with his new light and his practised training, were to publish a series of discourses on the leading doctrines of the gospel, these discourses would certainly be worth the reading, and would as certainly be read. Dr Huntington's is a parallel case to that exactly. We commend the volume very heartily to the attention of our readers."—*The Witness.*

"For freshness of thought, power of illustration, and evangelical earnestness, this writer is not surpassed by the ablest theologians in the palmiest days of the Church."—*Caledonian Mercury.*

"It is intrinsically a great book, abounding with fresh and scriptural thoughts, in which one may see the faith, and hope, and peace of a soul animated by the spirit of the gospel, and rejoicing in the sunlight of truth."—*The Christian Observer.*

"Everywhere through these pages there pulsates a genuine sincerity of conviction, which gives them a moral value and power beyond all reach of logical force, or of the most exquisite verbal felicities."—*The Independent.*

In Large Crown 8vo, Price 6s. Cloth,

BIBLE RECORDS OF REMARKABLE CONVERSIONS.

By the Rev. ADOLPH SAPHIR, Greenwich.

Extract from a Paper by JAMES HAMILTON, D.D., in *English Presbyterian Messenger.*

"With its deep insight, its glowing tone of love and gladness, and its abundance of thought, original, wise, and beautiful, this is a rare and remarkable book. Mr Saphir is a 'householder who bringeth forth out of his treasure things new and old;' and whilst he secures our confidence by his loyalty to the unchanging verities, he deserves our gratitude for many new and happy applications. Nor do we know many books where so much scholarship is brought to bear with so little ostentation, nor many books adapted to so wide a range of readers."

ALEXANDER STRAHAN & CO.,

THE TWENTIETH THOUSAND,

Price 6d., Sewed, of

WEE DAVIE.

By NORMAN MACLEOD, D.D.,
AUTHOR OF "THE OLD LIEUTENANT AND HIS SON," "THE EARNEST STUDENT," &c.

" 'Wee Davie' is a tale of real life, simple in style, unexciting in incident, plain in meaning, but richly embued with that charm of nature's truth and nature's pathos, which is the most powerful of literary spells. Readers ought to acquaint themselves with this exquisite little story."—*The Dial.*

"The beautiful little story of 'Wee Davie' was originally published in that repository of excellent writing, *Good Words*. It is one that few men but Dr, or, as he is affectionately and proudly called in Scotland, Norman Macleod, could write. 'Wee Davie' is the best exposition of the religion of affection that it has ever been our good fortune to read."—*Bedford Advertiser.*

"Fraught with the truest poetry, rich in divine philosophy, unapproachably the chief among productions of its class—this and more, is the story of 'Wee Davie.' By all means let every family have a copy of Dr Macleod's inimitable Christian tale, which is as powerful a preacher of the gospel as we have ever encountered."—*Dublin Warder.*

" 'Wee Davie' should be read by every man, woman, and child in every household in the land; and if the author had written nothing else, it would have stamped him as a master."—*Hawick Advertiser.*

"A most touching and beautiful story; every way worthy of the noble heart and mind which has here and elsewhere laid us under great obligations. It may soften and heal and guide many who much need a hearty and friendly voice to address them; and it will not be easy for any to read it with dry eyes. Get it, reader, and give it away when you have got the good out of it for yourself."—*Scottish Press.*

In Small Crown Octavo, Price 5s. Cloth,

THE RESTORATION OF THE JEWS:

THE HISTORY, PRINCIPLES, AND BEARINGS OF THE QUESTION.

By DAVID BROWN, D.D., Professor of Theology, Aberdeen, Author of "The Second Advent," &c. &c.

THE THIRD THOUSAND,

In Neat Cloth, Price 2s. 6d.,

THE AUTOCRAT OF THE BREAKFAST TABLE.

By OLIVER WENDELL HOLMES.

"I would rather be the Author of 'The Autocrat of the Breakfast Table' than of all Shelley's writings put together."—A. K. H. B. in *Fraser's Magazine*.

Workshop Tract by Norman Macleod, D.D.

Now Ready, in Shilling Packets of 15 Copies, for Distribution,

JOB JACOBS AND HIS BOXES.

A STORY ILLUSTRATIVE OF THE BENEFIT OF SAVINGS BANKS AND FRIENDLY SOCIETIES.

In Demy Octavo, Price 5s. Cloth,

THE REPORT OF THE PROCEEDINGS OF THE GENEVA CONFERENCE OF THE EVANGELICAL ALLIANCE.

EDITED BY THE REV. GAVIN CARLYLE, M.A.,
Editor of *The News of the Churches.*

Among the Contents of this Volume are the following Papers:—

Calvin and the Reformation in Geneva. By Dr MERLE D'AUBIGNE.
Ragged Schools in Scotland. By THOMAS GUTHRIE, D.D.
Christian Fraternity and Christian Polemics. By COUNT DE GASPARIN.
Religious Liberty. By Dr E. PRESSENSE.
Revivals. By Rev. and Hon. BAPTIST NOEL, and Rev. Dr URWICK.
The Working Classes in France. By Professor ST HILAIRE.
Individualism. By Dr DORNER.
The Sabbath. By Dr ANDREW THOMSON.
Scepticism in France. By Dr NAVILLE.
Italy and the Gospel. By Pastor MEILLE.
Romanism in America. By Rev. Dr BAIRD, New York.
The American War. By Dr MILES G. SQUIER.
Progress of Religion in Germany. By Pastor BONNET, and Dr THOLUCK.
Rationalism in German Switzerland. By Dr RIGGENBACH.
With Addresses by SIR CULLING EARDLEY, Drs KRUMMACHER, GRANDPIERRE, GAUSSEN, KALKAR, GROEN, VAN PRINTSTERER, MAZZARELLA, HERZOG; E. BAINES, Esq., M.P., &c.

SIXTY-SEVENTH THOUSAND,

In Neat Cloth, Price 1s. 6d.,

THE POWER OF PRAYER.
BY THE REV. DR PRIME.

TWENTY-SECOND THOUSAND,

In Neat Cloth, Price 1s. 6d.,

THE HIGHER CHRISTIAN LIFE.
BY THE REV. W. E. BOARDMAN.

TWENTIETH THOUSAND
is Now Ready of

THE STILL HOUR.

By AUSTIN PHELPS, D.D.

Fine Edition, 1s. ; Cheap Edition, 6d.

THIRTY-SECOND THOUSAND
is Now Ready of

BLIND BARTIMEUS AND HIS GREAT PHYSICIAN.

By the Rev. W. J. HOGE.

Fine Edition, 2s. 6d. ; Cheap Edition, 1s.

THIRTEENTH THOUSAND
is Now Ready of

THE WAY HOME.

By the Rev. W. BULLOCK.

In Neat Cloth, Price 1s. 6d.

THIRD THOUSAND
is Now Ready of

DAILY MEDITATIONS.

In Neat Cloth, Price 2s.

SIXTH THOUSAND
is Now Ready of

FORTY YEARS' EXPERIENCE OF SUNDAY SCHOOLS.

By STEPHEN H. TYNG, D.D.

In Neat Cloth, Price 1s. 6d.

Price Sixpence, Monthly,

THE NEWS OF THE CHURCHES
AND JOURNAL OF MISSIONS.

Supplying, Monthly, a Catholic and Comprehensive Account of all the Religious and Missionary Movements occurring throughout the whole World.

The Rev. Dr MILLER, of Birmingham, Canon of Worcester, &c.
"I should be glad could it find its way to the table, not only of every Christian minister, but of every Christian man."

The Hon. ARTHUR KINNAIRD, M.P.
"Most sincerely do I wish increased success to this valuable periodical."

E. B. UNDERHILL, Esq., Secretary of the Baptist Missionary Society.
"The *News of the Churches* stands alone among periodicals, as presenting in one view the progress of Divine truth in all lands. It deserves the great success it has already attained. I trust that success will yet be greater."

The Rev. JAMES H. RIGG, Author of "Modern Anglican Theology."
"There are few periodicals which I value more highly than the *News of the Churches*, or which I read with more interest and attention. It is unique in its character and purpose."

The Rev. Dr GUTHRIE.
"I consider the *News of the Churches* to be a most interesting, as it is a most catholic periodical. It is admirably conducted, and deserves the widest circulation."

The Rev. Dr NORMAN MACLEOD, Glasgow.
"I like well this monthly review of the grand army of the Church of Christ throughout the world; and not only find it pleasant and useful for myself, but for those also who attend my Sabbath-evening missionary prayer-meetings, when I always quote largely from its pages. I cordially recommend it, as catholic in its spirit, accurate in its information, and judicious in its selection of facts."

The Rev. Dr CANDLISH.
"The *News of the Churches* is a periodical fitted to meet a great want in the religious world. It is admirably conducted, being at once catholic and comprehensive on the one hand, and evangelical and spiritual on the other."

"Good words are worth much and cost little."—HERBERT.

MONTHLY PARTS, PRICE 6D.,

Profusely Illustrated with Woodcuts from Designs by

MILLAIS, HOLMAN HUNT, TENNIEL, WATSON, KEENE, WALKER, WOLF.

GOOD WORDS,

EDITED BY NORMAN MACLEOD, D.D.

Contents of the January Part.

1. A Word in Season. By the Editor.
2. The Facts and Fancies of Mr Darwin. By Sir David Brewster.
3. Out of Doors in January. By the Countess de Gasparin. Illustrated by J. D. Watson.
4. At Sea in Winter. By William Hansard, Sailor. Illustrated by Audrews.
5. Concerning the Reasonableness of Certain Words of Christ. By A. K. H. B., Author of "The Recreations of a Country Parson."
6. Olaf the Sinner and Olaf the Saint. By H. K. Illustrated by J. E. Millais.
7. The Union of Man with Man. A Present Day Paper. By Norman Macleod, D.D., Editor.
8. Food. By Archbishop Whately.
9. Go and Come. By Dora Greenwell. Illustrated by Holman Hunt.
10. Mistress and Maid. Chaps. I. and II. By the Author of "John Halifax, Gentleman." Illustrated by J. E. Millais.
11. All about the Indigo. By Thomas Smith, A.M., late of Calcutta. With Illustrations.
12. Above the Clouds. By Professor C. Piazzi Smyth, Astronomer-Royal for Scotland. Three Illustrations.
13. The Christmas Child. By Isa Craig. Illustrated by Morten.
14. At Home in the Scriptures. A Series of Family Readings. By the Rev. William Arnot.
15. Our Widowed Queen. By W. H. Latchmore.

Contents of the February Part.

1. Moments in Life. By the Editor.
2. Days and Nights in Greenland. By David Walker, M.D., F.R.G.S., F.L.S. With Four Illustrations by the Author.
3. The Worse the Better. By the Rev. Hugh Stowell Brown.
4. Old Customs and Old Folk. By the Countess de Gasparin, Author of "The Near and Heavenly Horizons." Illustrated by J. D. Watson.
5. The Battle of Gilboa. By the Author of "Kelavane." Illustrated by J. Tenniel.
6. The Blessings of those who Weep. By the late Rev. Edward Irving.
7. Gifts. A Parable from Nature. By Mrs Gatty.
8. Mistress and Maid. Chaps. III. and IV. By the Author of "John Halifax, Gentleman." Illustrated by J. E. Millais.
9. My Photographic Album. By Ann Warrender. Illustrated by T. B. Dalziel (from a Photograph.)
10. The Uses of the Moon. By Principal Leitch.
11. The Newspaper. By M. B.
12. The Carrier Pigeon. By Dora Greenwell. Illustrated by T. Morten.
13. At Home in the Scriptures. By the Rev. William Arnot.

Contents of the March Part.

1. What if Christianity is not True? By the Editor.
2. Three Lives Worth Knowing about. By the Rev. W. F. Stevenson.
3. Causes and Remedies of Colliery Calamities. By J. R. Leifchild.
4. A Cast in the Waggon. By Miss Sarah Tytler, Author of "Papers for Thoughtful Girls." Illustrated by J. D. Watson. Part I.
5. Rung into Heaven. By Horace Moule. Illustrated by M. J. Lawless.
6. Concerning Atmospheres. With some Thoughts on Currents. By A. K. H. B., Author of "Recreations of a Country Parson."
7. Mistress and Maid. Chaps. V. and VI. By the Author of "John Halifax, Gentleman." Illustrated by J. E. Millais.
8. The Eye: Its Structure and Powers. By Sir David Brewster. With Eight Illustrative Diagrams.
9. A Year of the Slavery Question in the United States (1859-60.) By J. Malcolm Ludlow.
10. Love in Death. By Dora Greenwell. Illustrated by Fred. Walker.
11. At Home in the Scriptures. By the Rev. William Arnot.

Contents of the April Part.

1. Sunday. By the Editor.
2. Short Papers. By Archbishop Whately. I. Hope and Fear. II. Influence.
3. Pictures in the Fire. By Gerald Massey. Illustrated by T. Morten.
4. A Cast in the Waggon. By Miss Sarah Tytler, Author of "Papers for Thoughtful Girls." Illustrated by J. D. Watson. Part II.
5. Colliers in their Homes and at their Work. By J. B. Leifchild. With Seven Illustrations.
6. What a Working Man said the other Day at the Opening of a Dissenting School in Hertfordshire. Reported by Himself in a Letter to a Friend.
7. Mistress and Maid. Chaps VII., VIII., and IX. By the Author of "John Halifax, Gentleman." Illustrated by J. E. Millais.
8. A Day in the Woods of Jamaica. By Philip Henry Gosse.
9. Time and its Measurement. By Professor C. Piazzi Smyth, Astronomer-Royal for Scotland. With an Illustration by the Author.
10. King Sigurd, the Crusader. A Norse Saga. By the Author of "The Martyrdom of Kelavane." Illustrated by E. B. Jones.
11. At Home in the Scriptures. By the Rev. William Arnot.

Contents of the May Part.

1. Missions in the Nineteenth Century. By the Editor.
2. What Sent Me to Sea. By Wm. Hansard. Illustrated by J. Pettie.
3. Wardie—Spring-Time. By Alex. Smith. With Two Illustrations by W. P. Burton.
4. Concerning Beginnings and Ends. By A. K. H. B., Author of "Recreations of a Country Parson."
5. Moshesh, the Chief of the Mountain. By J. M. Ludlow. With an Illustration.
6. Mistress and Maid. Chaps. X. and XI. By the Author of "John Halifax. Gentleman." Illustrated by J. E. Millais.
7. Old Maids and Young Maids. By the Author of "Memoirs of an Unknown Life."
8. The Crimson Flower. By the Countess de Gasparin, Author of "The Near and Heavenly Horizons." Illustrated by J. D. Watson.
9. Church Scandal in Rome in the Third Century. By Principal Tulloch.
10. Is He Stingy? By James Knox.
11. "Until Her Death." By the Author of "John Halifax, Gentleman." Illustrated by F. Sandys.
12. At Home in the Scriptures. By the Rev. William Arnot.

Contents of the June Part.

1. Five Shillings' worth of the Great World's Fair. By the Author of "John Halifax, Gentleman."
2. May-Day, 1862. An Ode. By Isa Craig.
3. Three Present-Day Tracts. By the Editor.
4. How an Irish Girl raised the Factory. With an Illustration.
5. On Glaciers. The First of Two Parts. By Principal Forbes. Illustrated.
6. God's Hand in the Paddle-Power of England. A Lecture delivered in a Hertfordsh. Dissenting Schoolroom.
7. Mistress and Maid. Chaps. XII. and
XIII. By the Author of "John Halifax, Gentleman." Illustrated by J. E. Millais.
8. An Essay on an Old Essayist—Montaigne. By Alexander Smith.
9. The Summer Woods. By William Forsyth. Illustrated by F. Walker.
10. On Some Guessers at Truth. By S. W. With an Illustration.
11. Summer Evening. By John Hollingshead. Illustrated by W. P. Burton.
12. At Home in the Scriptures. By the Rev. William Arnot.

Contents of the July Part.

1. Four Difficulties Solved in Jesus Christ. By the Editor.
2. Highland Flora. Illustrated by J. E. Millais.
3. An Exhibition Homily. By the Rev. J. Ll. Davis.
4. The East. By the Countess de Gasparin, Author of "The Near and Heavenly Horizons." Illustrated by J. D. Watson.
5. On Glaciers. The Second of Two Parts. By Principal Forbes. With Illustrations.
6. Horses and Homes. By Dr W. T. Gairdner.
7. Mistress and Maid. Chaps. XIV. and XV. By the Author of "John Halifax, Gentleman." Illustrated by J. E. Millais.
8. Matthew Claudius, Homme de Lettres. By W. Fleming Stevenson.
9. Some Verses Written by a Working-Man for the Children to Sing at an Anniversary Meeting in Hertfordshire. Illustrated by J. D. Watson.
10. Outside. By A. K. H. B., Author of "The Recreations of a Country Parson."
11. At Home in the Scriptures. By the Rev. William Arnot.

Contents of the August Part.

1. Rambling Notes on a Rambling Tour. By the Editor.
2. Vistas in the Russian Church. The First of Two Papers. By Professor C. Piazzi Smyth. With Two Illustrations.
3. Wickliffe's Version of the New Testament. By the Rev. Hugh S. Brown.
4. Our Neighbour. By the Editor.
5. On Solitude. By Æneas Sage. Illustrated by F. Stone.
6. Albert's Tomb. By Gerald Massey.
7. Mistress and Maid. Chaps. XVI., XVII., and XVIII. By the Author of "John Halifax, Gentleman." Illustrated by J. E. Millais.
8. Pages from my Note-Book. By Archbishop Whately.
9. The Human Eye: Its Phenomena and Illusions. By Sir D. Brewster.
10. My Treasure. Illustrated by A. B. Houghton.
11. At Home in the Scriptures. By the Rev. William Arnot.

Contents of the September Part.

1. A Peep at the Netherlands and Holland. By the Editor.
2. How Wondrous are Thy Works, O God! A Hymn. By John S. Blackie. Illustrated by W. P. Burton.
3. Geffrard, President of Hayti. By J. M. Ludlow.
4. Vistas in the Russian Church. Part II. By Professor Piazzi Smyth. With an Illustration.
5. Her Majesty Nannerl, the Washerwoman. By A. S. Illust. by Keene.
6. Getting on. By A. K. H. B.
7. Mistress and Maid. Chaps. XIX. and XX. By the Author of "John Halifax, Gentleman." Illustrated by J. E. Millais.
8. At Night in an Observatory. By Principal Leitch. With an Illustration.
9. Colonel Richard Baird Smith, C.B. By the Rev. Thomas Smith, A.M. With Portrait.
10. A True Ghost Story. (Dedicated to Spiritualists.) By the Editor.
11. Sea-Weeds. Illust. by H. Armstead.
12. At Home in the Scriptures. By the Rev. William Arnot.

ALEXANDER STRAHAN & CO.,

In One Elegant Volume of 750 Royal-Octavo Pages, Extra Cloth, Full Gilt, Price 7s. 6d.,

GOOD WORDS

FOR 1861.

EDITED BY NORMAN MACLEOD, D.D.,

And Illustrated with Eighty Wood Engravings, printed on Toned and White Paper.

The Publishers respectfully direct attention to the FOUR IMPORTANT NEW WORKS *which are published in this Volume.*

I.

THE RELIGION OF LIFE ILLUSTRATED AND APPLIED.

BY THOMAS GUTHRIE, D.D., EDINBURGH.

II.

THE OLD LIEUTENANT AND HIS SON.

BY NORMAN MACLEOD, D.D., EDITOR.

III.

OUR SUNDAY EVENINGS

A SERIES OF PAPERS FOR FAMILY READING, BY

JAMES HAMILTON, D.D.
A. P. STANLEY, D.D.
W. L. ALEXANDER, D.D.
DAVID BROWN, D.D.
REV. THOMAS BINNEY.
REV. W. M. PUNSHON.

JOHN EADIE, LL.D., D.D.
J. M. M'CULLOCH, D.D.
J. R. MACDUFF, D.D.
REV. THOMAS SMITH, A.M.
ROBERT LEE, D.D.
NORMAN MACLEOD, D.D.

IV.

ILLUSTRATIONS OF SCRIPTURE.

BY J. B.

Twelve full-page Illustrations, engraved by DALZIEL BROTHERS, and printed on Toned Paper.

Good Words for 1861—continued.

The following list of Papers will serve to indicate the General Contents of this Volume:—

Give us Air. By the Author of "John Halifax."
The Original Ragged School. "How it was Got up, and What it has Done." By Thomas Guthrie, D.D., Edinburgh.
Wee Davie. By Norman Macleod, D.D.
The Doctor. By John Brown, M.D., Author of "Rab and his Friends." 1. Our Duties to the Doctor. 2. The Doctor's Duties to Us. 3. Health. 4. Children, and How to Guide them. 5. Medical Odds and Ends.
The Light of the World. By Adolph Saphir.
Honesty is the Best Policy. By Hugh Stowell Brown.
The Working Associations of Paris. By J. M. Ludlow.
The Paradise of Fools. By J. H. Fyfe.
What is a Pound? By J. Hollingshead.
An Hour among the Torbay Sponges. By P. H. Gosse, F.R.S.
A Sabbath at Aldershott. By J. R. Macduff, D.D.
Cain's Brand. By H. K.
The First Look Out on the World. By the Author of "John Halifax."
The Life and History of a Salmon. By the Rev. David Esdaile.
The South-Sea Islands. 1. As they were Twenty Years ago. 2. As they are To-day. By the Rev. John Inglis, Missionary to the New Hebrides.
A Journey through Space. By Principal Leitch.
The House of Mirth. By the late Rev. Edward Irving.
The Waker, the Dreamer, and the Sleeper. By the Rev. J. de Liefde, Amsterdam.
Facts from a South Staffordshire Ragged School. By the Rev. H. W. Holland, Author of "Thieves and Thieving."
The Ever-Shining Stars. By Isaac Taylor.
My First Geological Excursion. By Archibald Geikie, F.G.S.
Memoirs of an Unknown Life. By an Unknown Author.
A Peep at Russia and the Shores of the Baltic. By Norman Macleod, D.D.
Pictures from the Early Life of the Church. By Principal Tulloch.
Eastern Prisons. By Thomas Smith, A.M., Calcutta.
T. T. Fitzroy, Esq. By Norman Macleod, D.D.
A National Song. By Dora Greenwell.

Street Scenes in Canton. By an Officer in the Royal Navy.
The Ways and Works of the Blind. By J. H. Fyfe.
What Have You Done? By Norman Macleod, D.D.
Goby Hunting. By P. H. Gosse, F.R.S.
Telescopes and Astronomers. By Principal Leitch.
The Cerealia: A Standing Miracle. By Professor Harvey.
The Ball of Worsted. By the Author of "Memoirs of an Unknown Life."
The Bee-Hive Close. By the Countess de Gasparin, Author of "The Near and Heavenly Horizons."
Flowers for the Poor. By the Rev. J. Erskine Clark.
St John of the East Sea. By W. F. Stevenson.
Missionary Enterprise in Equatorial Africa. By the Rev. A. Bushnell, Resident Missionary in the Gorilla Country.
The Man of War and the Parish School. By the Rev. W. G. Blaikie.
Short Papers for the Times. By Archbishop Whately.
All About the House. By Margaret Maria Gordon.
Deaconess Institution of Kaiserswerth. By William Fleming Stevenson.
London Model Lodging-Houses. By John Hollingshead.
The Coming of the Spring. By the Author of "John Halifax."
Scenes from the Life and Travels of our Lord. By the Rev. J. L. Porter, Author of "Murray's Handbook of Palestine."
Light and Scenery as Affecting Health. By Dr Angus Smith, Manchester.
The Wonder of Indifference. By Norman Macleod, D.D.
Peter Floger, the Tailor of Buinen. By the Rev. J. de Liefde, Amsterdam.
Patent Medicines. By Thos. H. Jones.
Village Incidents. By Elsie Garret.
Bees and the Art of Queen-Making. By Principal Leitch.
The Creation of the World. By John Stuart Blackie, Professor of Greek in the University of Edinburgh.
The Emancipation of the Serfs. By C. Orischinsky, St Petersburg.
Books of Devotion. By W. F. Stevenson.
The Strange Origin of the Friesland Cap. A Legend of Holland. By the Rev. J. de Liefde, Amsterdam.

In One Elegant Volume of 800 Royal-Octavo Pages, Extra Cloth,
Full Gilt, Price 7s. 6d.,

GOOD WORDS
FOR 1860.
EDITED BY NORMAN MACLEOD, D.D.,

And Illustrated with 102 *Wood Engravings from Designs by Eminent Artists.*

Among the Authors are—

The Rev. J. CAIRD, D.D., Glasgow.
Miss MULOCK, Author of "John Halifax, Gentleman."
Dr MERLE D'AUBIGNE, Geneva.
Professor DAVID BROWN, Aberdeen.
The Author of the "Nut-Brown Maidens."
GERALD MASSEY.
The Rev. W. MORLEY PUNSHON.
The Rev. JOHN CUMMING, D.D.

Mrs MARGARET MARIA GORDON.
The Rev. HUGH STOWELL BROWN.
Principal TULLOCH.
The Rev. J. DE LIEFDE, Amsterdam, Author of "The Pastor of Gegenburg."
The Rev. J. R. MACDUFF, D.D.
Principal LEITCH.
Miss MARSH.
The Rev. NORMAN MACLEOD, D.D.

Among the Artists are—

JAMES ARCHER, R.S.A.
JAMES DRUMMOND, R.S.A.
ERSKINE NICOL, R.S.A.
GOURLAY STEELL, R.S.A.
SAMUEL BOUGH.
CLARK STANTON.

WILLIAM Q. ORCHARDSON.
JOHN MACWHIRTER.
CLARENCE DOBELL.
ROBERT HERDMAN.
C. A. DOYLE.
KEELEY HALSWELLE.

Among the Contributions are—

GOD'S GLORY IN THE HEAVENS. 10 Chapters.
By PRINCIPAL LEITCH.

COUNSELS FOR YOUNG MEN. 4 Chapters.
By NORMAN MACLEOD, D.D., EDITOR.

MEDITATIONS ON HEAVEN. 7 Chapters.
By the Rev. J. R. MACDUFF, D.D., Author of the "Morning and Night Watches."

LADY SOMERVILLE'S MAIDENS. A Story. 29 Chapters.
By the Author of the "Nut-Brown Maidens."

THE GOLD THREAD. A Story for the Young. 5 Chapters.
By NORMAN MACLEOD, D.D., EDITOR.

DAILY MEDITATIONS; or, Good Words for Every Day
(365 Readings).

Good Words for 1860—continued.

Pictures from the Life of the Early Church. Three Chapters. By Principal Tulloch.
Aspects of Indian Life during the Rebellion. Six Papers. By J. M. Ludlow, Esq.
Photographs from the Gospels. Three Chapters. By Professor David Brown.
Missionary Sketches. Six Papers. By Thomas Smith, A.M.
Christian Life in Germany in the Nineteenth Century. Ten Chapters. By W. F. Stevenson.
Bible Records of Remarkable Conversions. Three Papers. By Adolph Saphir.
Joy among the Angels. By Rev. W. Landels.
Song of Antioch. By J. M. Ludlow, Esq.
Incident in the Arctic Seas. By Rev. J. R. Macduff, D.D.
On the Atlantic. By Norman Macleod, D.D.
Auroras. By W. Jack, of St Peter's Hall, Cambridge.
The Caravansary of Bagdad, from the Danish.
Bees and Bee-Hives. By John Cumming, D.D.
The Destroyed Cities of the Plain. By the Rev. Dr Jamieson.
St Columbia. By Professor Shairp, St Andrews.
Concerning Childhood. By Geo. Hume.
Illustrations of Providence. By Canon Stowell.
Doctor Sparrow. By Adolph Saphir.
A Summer's Study of Ferns. By Miss Fernlover.
1515 versus 1860. By Dr M. D'Aubigne.
What has been done in the Fiji Islands. By Miss Farmer.
Protestantism in France. By Principal Tulloch.
The Fate of Franklin. By J. M.
A Summer Hour in my Garden. By George Hume.
How I became a Governess. By Miss —
The Evils of Great Cities. By A. T. I.
The Crowded Harbour. By Miss Marsh, Author of "Memorials of Hedley Vicars."
A Door Opened in Heaven. By Professor David Brown.
Highlanders at Home and Abroad. By Norman Macleod, D.D.

Professor George Wilson. By W. Lindsay Alexander, D.D.
Scenes in Itlay. By Wm. Arthur, A.M.
Latimer in the Pulpit. By Hugh Stowell Brown.
The True Rest for Man. By Norman Macleod, D.D.
David Chart's Memoranda. By Miss Howitt.
Methodism in the Far West. By W.H.G.
Ascent of Mont Blanc. By a Member of the Alpine Club.
Sketches in Natural History. By Wm. Keddie.
The Midnight Mission. By L. C. C.
The Story of Ninian. By Professor Shairp.
Nuremberg Stories. By Adolph Saphir.
Our Bob. By Norman Macleod, D.D.
A String of Pearls. By the Rev. Dr M'Farlane, Author of "The Night Lamp."
The Power of Prayer. By W. F. Stevenson.
Concerning Each One's Religious History. By A. T. I.
Saul of Tarsus a Chosen Vessel. By the Rev. Dr M'Culloch.
The Little Screw. By the Rev. J. de Liefde, Amsterdam, Author of "The Pastor of Gegenburg."
Popular Misapplications of Scripture. By Hugh Stowell Brown.
The Broken Link. By Mrs Margaret Maria Gordon.
Old Jenny of Glen Immern. By Norman Macleod, D.D.
In the Life of a Village Schoolmaster. By W. F. Stevenson.
Reflections of a Rifle Volunteer. By A. T. I.
Symbolism in the Christian Economy. By John Caird, D.D.
Journey by Sinai to Syria. By the Rev. Donald Macleod.
Massacre of Christians in Syria, By Professor J. L. Porter, Author of "Murray's Handbook of Palestine."
The Little Rift. By L. C. C.
Alexander von Humboldt. By the Rev. Dr Hoffman, Royal Chaplain, Berlin.
An Autumn Psalm. By the Author of "John Halifax, Gentleman."
Garibaldi. By Gerald Massey.
The Lone One. By H. Mary T.
The White Crusade—Italy, 1860. By the Author of "The Patience of Hope."

ALEXANDER STRAHAN & CO.

"Good words are worth much and cost little."—HERBERT.

MONTHLY PARTS, PRICE 6D.,

Profusely Illustrated with Woodcuts from Designs by
MILLAIS, HOLMAN HUNT, TENNIEL, WATSON, KEENE, WALKER, WOLF.

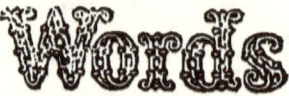

EDITED BY NORMAN MACLEOD, D.D.,
ONE OF HER MAJESTY'S CHAPLAINS FOR SCOTLAND.

THOMAS GUTHRIE, D.D.,
(AUTHOR OF "THE GOSPEL IN EZEKIEL," ETC.,)
Is preparing a New Work to be published in GOOD WORDS for 1863.
To commence in January and be completed in December.

JOHN CAIRD, D.D.,
(AUTHOR OF "THE RELIGION OF COMMON LIFE," ETC.,)
Is preparing a New Work to be published in GOOD WORDS for 1863.
To commence in January and be completed in December.

ANTHONY TROLLOPE,
(AUTHOR OF "FRAMLEY PARSONAGE," ETC.,)
Is preparing a New Story to be published in GOOD WORDS for 1863.

JOHN E. MILLAIS, A.R.A.,
Will contribute TWELVE ILLUSTRATIONS OF THE PARABLES
to GOOD WORDS for 1863.
They will be Engraved by DALZIEL BROTHERS, and Printed on Toned Paper.

www.ingramcontent.com/pod-product-compliance
Lightning Source LLC
Chambersburg PA
CBHW021409230426
43666CB00006B/690